Guiding *the* Faith Journey

A Map For Spiritual Leaders

NEIL DE KONING

CRC Publications
Grand Rapids, Michigan

Author Neil de Koning is pastor of Redeemer Christian Reformed Church in Sarnia, Ontario.

Images ©1996 PhotoDisc, Inc.

Guiding the Faith Journey, © 1996, CRC Publications, 2850 Kalamazoo Ave. SE, Grand Rapids, MI 49560.

Library of Congress Cataloging in Publication Data

De Koning, Neil, 1953–
    Guiding the faith journey : a map for spiritual leaders / Neil de Koning.
      p. cm.
    Includes bibliographical references.
    ISBN 1-56212-178-2
    1. Spiritual life—Christian Reformed Church. 2. Spiritual direction. 3. Christian Reformed Church—Membership. 4. Reformed Church—Membership. I. Title.
BX6826.D45 1996
248.4'85731—dc20

96-14885
CIP

10 9 8 7 6 5 4 3 2

Table of Contents

Preface

Leaders in the church are given a high calling by God to guide people in their walk with the Lord. Yet few enter this calling trained and ready. This book is intended to help those called to be spiritual guides to develop the gifts and wisdom they need.

Nurturing these gifts and gaining wisdom is a lifelong journey of faith for those called to lead. It always begins with listening to God. The Spirit illumines our hearts and directs our paths. It is a communal journey in which we listen to the wisdom of our brothers and sisters, stretch our understanding, and nurture our gifts.

This book is intended to be used in a group of those called to be spiritual guides. In my congregation, elders are called to be spiritual guides. In other congregations, this group may include small group leaders.

Because spiritual nurturing is a lifelong journey, this book is intended to be used over time. For example, in my congregation an elder's term of office is three years. If the book is divided into bite-sized chunks, it can form a basis for discussion over an elder's entire term of office.

I suggest the following:

A retreat at the beginning of the year

Focus: Year 1—Chapters 1, 3

          Year 2—Chapters 2, 4

          Year 3—Chapters 5, 6

An hour at two regularly scheduled meetings in the fall

Focus: Year 1—Chapters 7, 9

          Year 2—Chapters 8, 12

          Year 3—Chapters 10, 11

An hour at two regularly scheduled meetings in the winter

Focus: Year 1—Chapters 13, 16

          Year 2—Chapters 14, 17

          Year 3—Chapters 15, 19

This schedule is only a suggestion. Adjust it to your needs. If something is missing, add your own chapter. Remember, this is a journey we are on together. Together we seek to respond to God's call and guidance in our lives.

Part One

Spiritual Guides:
Developing Gifts for Ministry

One day I realized others were listening to me as if I were saying something valuable. It was a scary thought. I had not considered my insight that unique nor my contributions in discussions of much significance. Suddenly, I was discovering the real possibility that my words might influence another person's relationship with God.

The prospect raised many questions. The truth we know about ourselves only increases our doubts. How can I help others pray when I struggle in my own prayer life? What can I say to help another person when I am only beginning to comprehend the movements of my heart? What wisdom can I share when I have only scratched the surface of biblically inspired understanding?

Yet here we are. We have heard God's call to service. The voices of our sisters and brothers have deepened our realization that God wants us to help others in the journey of faith. Now is the time to develop our calling.

What training ought I undergo to develop my gifts? How do I develop my understanding of the work of the Holy Spirit in a person's life? How do I listen to God's leading in the practice of ministry?

In Part One we look at ourselves. Through our attention to our own development, we grow in our ability to serve others.

Chapter 1

Introduction

"In the beginning, God . . ."

My journey of faith began before I found words to tell the story. God formed me in my mother's womb. In the womb, God made me to enjoy his presence. Before I took my first step, there was space in my heart for God. Born into a family that loved the Lord, I heard the songs of faith and the prayers of the redeemed. When I was a young child, my parents read the stories of Scripture. I take no credit for any of this. My beginning in the journey of faith was rooted in God's creative and gracious Word of life. I benefited. I never knew a time when I did not know the Lord. For this I thank the Lord.

Not all share my story. Perhaps you learned your faith later in life. Perhaps, like the apostle Paul, you met Christ along the way and experienced a radical transformation. Or like Lydia, you met Jesus through the preaching of the gospel. However you started your journey of faith, it is equally rooted in God's creative and gracious Word.

Just as "the Lord opened [Lydia's] heart to respond to Paul's message" (Acts 16:14), the Lord opens our hearts to Christ. In the beginning of our journey of faith, God speaks a word of love. The seed of new life is given to us by the Holy Spirit.

> Exercise: In prayer time, read Isaiah 43:1-4. Because God saves you in Christ, such a promise also extends to you. Consider God's personal, creative, and gracious word to you. Write a brief account of your beginning in faith.

"We shall be like him. . ."

Not only does our journey have a beginning with God; it also will have an ending with God. Revelation speaks of a new creation in which God's people will find complete redemption. Our journey of faith will end in the new creation. I do not pretend to know what that world will look like. Yet Scripture reveals that this destiny expresses my deepest longings: love will flourish in all relationships; peace will be found in every place; all will be well. In the center of the love, joy, and peace, we will find Jesus Christ with the Father and the Spirit.

Exercise: Read Revelation 21:1-5. Imagine what it would be like in your home, your church, your school, and your workplace if pain and crying were not present and joy and peace were to become reality today. What would have to change? Who would have to change? How would you be different?

I long for such a time. Wouldn't it be wonderful if I felt at peace always? Yet too many times I feel harried and experience tension in the fellowship of believers. Wouldn't it be wonderful if forgiveness ruled my heart? Yet too many times my anger makes forgiveness difficult. Wouldn't it be wonderful if everyone experienced joy in worship? Yet too many times worship becomes a point of conflict. I long for a time of new creation, joy, peace, love, and worship. I wish the disorder and chaos I feel could be blamed on another's sins. But honesty leads me to confess that I am part of the problem. The sin and brokenness lodged deep in my soul disturb my peace and joy. So I long for a time when I can be more than all right. My God-given longings pull me toward the new creation in which I will be like Christ.

This destiny in Christ is a vital element of our journey. It is the direction to which our spiritual compasses point. It is our true North. We know where we are going. Scripture tells us that when Abraham was called, he obeyed and went, even though he did not know the place to which he was going. He did this because he was "looking forward to the city with foundations, whose architect and builder is God" (Heb. 11:10). Like Abraham, our destiny pulls us onward in our journey of faith.

Every year, several students leave our congregation to go to college. While parents send them on their way with love and tears, the students leave with excitement. The roads their cars follow and the dreams of their souls anticipate their destination. Like students pulled to college, our destiny in Christ pulls us toward our future.

"Work out your salvation. . ."

Somewhere between the good beginning and our eternal destiny in the new creation, we live our daily ordinary lives. As I write this, my son is practicing piano, my wife is setting the dinner table, my daughter is studying for a test, and I am wondering if what I write will be at all useful. There is a meeting tonight. The choir is getting ready for Sunday worship. The bulletin needs to be prepared. The phone rings. What does it mean to work out my salvation? What does it mean to nurture the new life that God has planted in my soul? What does it help to look to my future in a new creation? How can I be an imagebearer of Christ?

If I am honest, I realize that the present moment is filled with obligations and feelings that press on me. When I focus on the immediate, it is easy to forget the call of God. As Teresa of Avila prayed, so I pray: "Lord, I know that you are constantly beside me, yet I am usually so busy that I ignore you." Busyness is not the only cause for being forgetful about God. We can be so sad, or so filled with personal ambition, or so consumed with passion for a lover that our ordinary lives seem distant from the great calling to work out our salvation.

Exercise: Read Philippians 2. Face the tension you feel in your devotion and service to God. Write down three areas of concern you have.

So I turn away from my ordinary life. I devote myself to the work of the church, to the struggle for justice in the world, to support for Christian education. At least the relationship between such work and God's work of salvation seems a little clearer. Then new questions come: In what work should I participate? Should I spend my extra hours on the church council or with Habitat for Humanity? Should I get involved on the school board or stay home with my family? Should I go out this evening with friends from church or spend the evening at home with God? Even in these holy works, working out my salvation is not so clear.

The routines of my daily life, the press of my obligations, my personal history of brokenness, and the call of my daily occupation frequently compete with the God-directed longings of my heart. How do I bring my fractured life into a holy order? How can my divided heart find a holy simplicity? How can I say no to the church and yes to God? How does worship become worship and not just an activity on a busy Sunday? How do I decide in what activities I will be involved? This is the stuff of our spiritual journey. Along the way we seek to bring God greater glory.

"Each one has a manifestation of the Spirit for the common good. . ."

At times, our family enjoys hiking nature trails. If we have never been on a particular trail before, we wonder what the trail is like. Is it difficult? How long will the hike take? When we cross paths with another hiker, we stop for a moment to ask the inevitable questions about the path ahead. We share our experience, tell a story, or perhaps pass on a little advice.

Along the journey of faith, God has placed fellow travelers on our path. Sisters and brothers in Christ are given gifts to share with us. They have stories to tell of God's grace in their lives. Many have struggled as they have journeyed and matured in faith and life. Among them are those gifted with discernment to search out the way of the Spirit and the Word in our lives. Among them are those called to give leadership in the church of Christ. These are people called by the Lord to guide the church—the people of God—to maturity in faith and life.

You may be one of these people gifted and called by Christ and his church to help fellow travelers along the way. As a pastor, I see this calling as a great opportunity and an awesome task. In moments in which I see spiritual growth in a person's journey of faith, I am filled with thankfulness and joy for the opportunity God has given me to be a ministry of grace. Still I am amazed at the complexity of the human soul. I know the pitfalls into which I unwittingly fall. Usually I am left with many questions to which I seek answers.

In the pages that follow, I do not intend to give answers. With you I am looking for better eyes to see another's journey, better ears to hear another's story, and better questions to probe another's heart. With you I am searching for biblically inspired wisdom to teach us and guide us to maturity in Christ. It is my prayer that these chapters will help you develop your gift and calling from the Lord.

For the love of Christ and your brothers and sisters, do not neglect the gift or the calling you have received. Soli Deo Gloria!

Chapter 2

Do I Have What It Takes?

Often I am perplexed by the mystery of the human person.

The more I learn and see, the more I wonder: Do I really have what it takes to be a spiritual guide to the people I meet?

My experience is not unique. Many women came to Susan for a time of fellowship and conversation on spiritual matters. Her home was a safe place. When I visited her to ask about her work, she downplayed her role. It was not just humility; she felt inadequate. Many lives she touched were filled with turmoil. She wished she could do more. But often she did not know what to say or do. She felt the needs of those around her stretching her insight and heart into territories unknown.

Exercise: Name two people who were or are spiritual guides for you or others. How would they feel about being named? Do they have a sense of competence, or do they feel overwhelmed by this calling?

In elders' meetings I stopped being surprised by the confessions of inadequacy. Even the wisest find their abilities overwhelmed and their confidence undermined. Not surprisingly, those who begin the work of spiritual direction often wonder: Do I have what it takes?

Facing Our Limitations

Wondering about our qualifications for leading others in faith is understandable. Matters of the soul are not diagnosed with X rays or treated with drugs. What we do not know about people and the work of God's Spirit far outweighs what we do know. This is not because of lack of training or utter stupidity. We are simply facing the limitations of our knowledge and competence. We need to see this as a strength rather than as a disqualification.

Read Exodus 3 and Jeremiah 1. What are some limitations Moses and Jeremiah felt as they heard God's call? What was God's response?

A little knowledge can be a dangerous thing. Several weeks after a funeral, I visit with the family members. Frequently, we discuss the insensitive comments some have made (e.g., "It is God's will"). However well meant, the words are uncaring and unhelpful. They are usually offered by those who know a little theology and feel uncomfortable around death. They know too little about the perplexing issues of the will of God. They know too little about the turmoil inside the person they seek to

Exercise: When do you feel out of your depth in conversation? When are you overwhelmed by the circumstances of a person's life?

comfort. They know too little about their own souls. When they repeat the phrases they have heard without considering their impact, they use the little they know inappropriately, causing deep hurt.

Recognizing the limitations of our knowledge and the deep mysteries of our life is invaluable. Awe and humility make us better listeners, help us speak more carefully, and allow us to confess our mistakes more quickly. Facing our limitations can lead us to a deeper dependence on the Spirit's guidance.

Our sense of inadequacy at the mystery of life and the perplexing difficulties of the task of guiding others is the necessary humble beginning for this holy calling. In an act of trust, we embrace the Spirit who will guide us in our ministry.

God Qualifies Us

To the extent that God has moved us to walk with him, to pursue him in our daily journey through life, and to serve him faithfully, we have something to share with those around us. We share our faith and what God has taught us. We share our gifts and our love. We share our experience of the Spirit of God. What God has worked in our lives is the foundation for the calling of being a spiritual guide.

Being a spiritual guide is not so much a matter of competence as it is a matter of dependence on the work of the Spirit. It is the Spirit who gives life and sanctifies believers—ourselves and others. The Spirit is competent. Only as we are open to the work of God can we be useful in guiding others in their relationships with God.

Give three steps of God's Spirit leading you toward a ministry of helping others in their faith life.

With amazing grace, God chooses to use us and qualify us for ministry. Before I decided to go into the ministry, I reasoned that if God wanted me to study for the ministry I would have received the gift for language. This was clearly not the case—my French grades were proof of my foreign language inability, and my writing skills were dismal (thank God for editors!). But God was unfazed by my reasoning. Quietly, the Spirit kept nudging me toward the Lord's ambition for my life. Experiences of service, encouraging words of friends, the motivation of my heart, and the interests of my mind kept leading in one direction. Clearly, God had chosen long before *I* chose. I experienced the leading of the Spirit.

As the Spirit leads, I have discovered the truth of the parable of the talents: when we use God-given gifts, God blesses and multiplies the gifts we have. When God calls us to serve, God provides all we need. As we use the Lord's provisions for the journey, the Spirit develops our gifts and even adds to them. God qualifies us.

We find our confidence in the assurance that the one who began the good work in us will continue to be with us as we embrace God's call to walk with others in their faith journey.

Exercise: Read Timothy 4:12-16. How did God qualify Timothy for ministry?

A World of Opportunity

I am amazed by the opportunities God gives us to journey with people. Sometimes the moment is brief. Like Philip with the Ethiopian eunuch, our conversation may touch on the heart of the gospel and the soul of the person very quickly. Then we are gone. But in that moment we have a powerful opportunity to lead a person to a deeper life with the Lord.

At other times, it takes years to develop a relationship of trust and love with a person. For whatever reason, someone's initial reaction to a conversation about God, grace, and the Spirit-filled life may be resistance. The subject of conversation may change. Silence may pervade the room. Yet God has placed this person on our path. In time, perhaps years, the resistance may diminish. God uses our love to pry open the door of the broken heart.

Give some examples of opportunities you have had to have spiritual conversations in your relationships with various people.

God also calls us into a situation in which our responsibilities give us opportunities to lead others to a deeper life with God. We become elders or Bible study leaders. We find ourselves leading a youth group. We chair a committee or become part of a visitation team. Responsibilities give us opportunities. Through them, Christ chooses to use us to deepen relationships with God.

Do I Have What It Takes?

Here is a trustworthy saying: If anyone sets his heart on being an overseer, he desires a noble task.

1 Timothy 3:1

Setting our hearts on this task of spiritual direction can seem very arrogant. How can anyone claim to have what it takes to nurture another soul? Yet God chooses to work through people—to make us responsible for nurturing others. Parents nurture children. Spiritual guides nurture human souls. God may have chosen you as a spiritual guide.

At the beginning of this chapter, we raised a personal question: Do I have what it takes? Our response focuses our hearts on God: the Spirit of God, who has what it takes, calls me and gives me gifts for ministry. We accept this call.

Here I am, Lord.
Is it I, Lord?
I have heard you calling in the night.
I will go, Lord, if you lead me.
I will hold your people in my heart.

Chapter 3

Developing the Gifts: A Personal Journey

Developing gifts for providing spiritual direction involves more than cultivating a set of skills. Just as there is more to carpentry than the skill of swinging a hammer, there is more to helping others on their spiritual odyssey than the skill of listening.

The first training ground is our own experience: How do the words of Scripture dig into my life? What words should I use to talk about my relationship with Christ? How does the Spirit lead me to follow God's call in my life?

When giving spiritual direction, we apply the gospel of Christ to the life of a person called by God. To help others on their spiritual journey, we pay attention to our own spiritual journey with the Lord.

Telling Our Story

Julie was looking for hope when she asked me, "What do *you* need to have forgiven?" To her, my life seemed simple and uncomplicated. Her life was a story of brokenness, sin, and pain. Abuse had destroyed her childhood. Divorce had ripped apart an early marriage. Promiscuity had entered in recent years. Now she was on the way back into the arms of Christ. She knew God loved her. But she struggled with being loved. She knew God forgave her, yet she struggled with being forgiven. She wondered what it felt like. To her, I seemed to live an ideal life. How could I know her struggles with forgiveness? It was time to tell my story.

Such moments are frequent in spiritual direction. A cry comes from deep within the soul. No theological response is adequate. Simply quoting a few biblical texts provides little comfort. The words of Scripture and confessional insight must find a home in my own life. I must be a witness to the grace God has worked in my life. I must now face the same question I asked. How will I respond?

Exercise: Your story begins in your childhood. What makes your faith life different from that of your parents?

Exercise: What Bible story
has particular meaning for
you? Why? If you were to
choose a theme passage for
yourself, what passage
would you pick? Why?

To shape our response, we must reflect on our experience of God's presence. We tell our story in the light of Scripture. The Bible is the story of God's love for humanity. In these stories, the love of God is given a shape and form. From words of guidance to prophetic confrontations, from angry judgments to gracious words of forgiveness, Scripture opens our eyes to see God in action. Experiencing God's presence is different from having a mystical experience. All experience must be tested to see whether it is of God. Prayerful reflection on Scripture is the surest guide to a deeper understanding of God's action in our lives. We discover the ways of God's love to us. We learn what pleases God. As we hear the story of God's love, we discern the ways of God in this world.

For example, here is a story in John 8:2-11:

> At dawn he appeared again in the temple courts, where all the people gathered around him, and he sat down to teach them. The teachers of the law and the Pharisees brought in a woman caught in adultery. They made her stand before the group and said to Jesus, "Teacher, this woman was caught in the act of adultery. In the Law Moses commanded us to stone such women. Now what do you say?" They were using this question as a trap, in order to have a basis for accusing him. But Jesus bent down and started to write on the ground with his finger. When they kept on questioning him, he straightened up and said to them, "If any one of you is without sin, let him be the first to throw a stone at her." Again he stooped down and wrote on the ground. At this, those who heard began to go away one at a time, the older ones first, until only Jesus was left, with the woman still standing there. Jesus straightened up and asked her, "Woman, where are they? Has no one condemned you?" "No one, sir," she said. "Then neither do I condemn you," Jesus declared. "Go now and leave your life of sin."

In this story of God's love coming in an unexpected way, we discern the movement of God in the lives of people. God moved in the life of the woman, forgiving and healing. God moved in the life of the crowd, confronting them with their own sin and leading them to forgiven and grace-filled lives.

Such discernment helps us tell our story. Our reflections lead us to understand our personal experience of God's love. Forgiveness, for example, is more than a biblical or theological truth. Our sin needs to be forgiven. The sin that crouches at our doors, seeking to destroy us, needs to be overcome. This is a personal story shaped by the story of God's love.

The story in John 8 reveals different kinds of sins. Adultery was the obvious one. But didn't Jesus tell us that lust was just as damning? Isn't Jesus saying that the self-righteousness of the leaders was equally damning to their souls? What name would I give my own sin? How does lust enter my life? How does pride show itself in my life? What happens when the words of Jesus—"Neither do I condemn you"—touch my experience? How does this experience of God's acceptance shield me from the slings and arrows of those who point their fingers?

Julie deserves an answer that witnesses to the truth expressed in Scripture. She needs to know that *you* would be among those who *could not* cast a stone. She needs to hear Jesus say, "Neither do I condemn you. . . ," and she needs to know that this gospel of peace can give her the confidence to enter the most holy place as a person loved by God.

This is the essential first step. The critical task is simply telling the wonders and miracles of God in our lives and in the life of the community. The story begins in Scripture. But it continues as you see the power of the gospel touch your life and the lives of those around you. This awareness of God's presence today helps provide guidance to brothers and sisters in Christ.

When you share your story, you do not set yourself up as a shining example or as the perfect model to be imitated. You know too well that your own quirks and unique circumstances make easy comparisons impossible. Yet your experience of God's saving work in your life, humbly told, shows that you are a fellow traveler on the way. You also need to experience God's grace to carry on. You also live in hope. That's where your stories converge.

Developing the Disciplines

My grandfather left the house early in the morning to bring in the cows for milking time. On his journey from the field to the milking shed, he would sing the psalms he had learned in grade school. For him this was much more than love for song. It was a spiritual exercise. His heart found its true home with the Lord.

All those who wish to mature in their relationship with God partake of activities that encourage such growth. Scripture reading, prayer, singing, worship, and works of service are among such activities. If we want to meet God and deepen our relationship with him, we go to those places where we are likely to meet God. In reading Scripture, I put myself close to God's voice. In worship I can draw near to God. In serving in the kingdom of God, I can become busy with the very things with which God is busy. Other activities clearly distract us from God. Spending time watching a porn movie does nothing to build our relationship with God. Spending time partying does nothing to encourage spiritual growth. The activities that build my relationship with God need to be part of our regular daily life.

Exercise: Choose a discipline that needs improvement in your life. What is dissatisfying about it? What are you prepared to do about it?

To help others develop these activities in their lives, we need to develop them in ours. What we seek is a regular practice of living with the Lord. Good habits of spirituality build Christian maturity. But habits do not enter our lives automatically. They are developed and encouraged. When our lives change, good habits are jeopardized.

For example, many young people learned to read Scripture and pray with their families at the dinner table. The good habit is often lost when they eat in the commons in a college. Suddenly they discover that it takes determined effort to find quiet time for devotional reading. Changing work habits, a move to a new location, or a change in family circumstances can have an equally negative impact on our good habits and on our spirituality.

Note a few significant changes in your life. What effect have these changes had on your spiritual disciplines?

Our personal experience with God's guidance through the disciplines of our lives helps us develop the gifts of spiritual guidance. We become more deeply aware of the role they play in our lives. We learn to recognize God speaking to us. By God's grace, they shape our lives to the glory of God.

Chapter 4
The Art of Listening

Listening is a precious art. By it we honor the one who is speaking. However confused or inarticulate the person is, we value the person simply by paying attention to what is said. As we listen, we ask questions to gain a deeper understanding of what lives in the person's heart. Listening is an act of love that affirms and blesses the one being heard.

Doctors listen with an ear to the sickness of the body. Psychologists listen with an ear for emotional struggles of the heart. Spiritual guides also listen with a special ear—an ear for the spiritual journey. Believing that God is at work, spiritual guides seek to hear the story of God's presence.

In learning the art of listening, we seek to minimize all that prevents us from listening and to maximize the opportunities for others to speak from their hearts.

Exercise: Read Numbers 14. Twice Israel demonstrated an inability to listen. What made listening to God so difficult for them?

Minimizing Our Inattention

All of us experience times when listening is difficult. After a demanding council meeting, I find it hard to pay undivided attention to conversation at home. When I am getting ready to leave the house, a telephone conversation can be a great effort. If I believe that Mrs. Smith is simply whining, I have great difficulty treating her concerns with seriousness. Part of learning to listen well is facing our prejudices and preoccupations—all those affairs of the heart that turn us toward ourselves. We are never without them, yet there are times when these movements of our hearts so control our ears that we listen to satisfy our longings.

If I hunger for affection, I listen for any hint of love. If I feel that I am inadequate, I listen for words that affirm. If I am consumed with doing well financially, I listen for the stories of wealth and poverty. When I feel joy at the birth of my child, it is harder to focus on the pain of another. When death comes near to me, the pain of my own heart drowns out the voice of those who speak.

What fears do you recognize in your life? How do they affect your behavior? Your listening skills?

21

Whatever our particular concerns, they affect the ears with which we listen. To minimize our inattention, we acknowledge our concerns and discipline our hearts.

Acknowledging the movements of our hearts that can damage our ability to listen is a lifelong, deliberate project. It is unrealistic to suggest that we should analyze every conversation. But it is unwise never to reflect on our conversations. We want answers to some questions:

- Why do I avoid some subjects?

- Why do I avoid some people?

- Why do I get angry with some topics or people?

- Why do I get excited about other topics and people?

- Where was God in this conversation?

- Why did I feel insecure?

- What was the cause of my restlessness?

- Why did I feel revulsion?

The answers tell us about ourselves. We learn to see the things that block out the voices of others. By acknowledging these realities, we take the first step to being a better listening ear.

Using our insight and seeking the power of the Spirit in our lives, we discipline our hearts and ears to listen.

Maximizing Our Attention

A good listener provides people with the opportunity to speak. It begins with making space for conversation.

One evening at seven-thirty, I arrived to visit Sarah and Peter, young parents who wanted their daughter baptized. The child was being fed. The television was on. Although I had come by arrangement, they didn't seem ready.

I arrived at John's office at lunchtime. He closed the door and arranged for us to not be interrupted. We were ready to talk and listen.

Essential to good listening is a hospitable space. Some people feel safe and comfortable in a restaurant. Others feel better around the kitchen table with a cup of coffee. Yet others need a quiet, secluded place where they can relax. We need a hospitable space and time where our hearts can open up to each other and to God.

Once in that space, a good listener asks questions. Open-ended questions help deepen the conversation. Such questions do not just ask for a yes or no response: "Is your spiritual life OK?" They do not lock a person into a predetermined response: "So I can safely report back to council that your spiritual life is OK?" An open-ended question creates room: "How have you sensed God working in your life since we last talked?" Most often, our talk begins superficially, but good questions draw our conversation to the matters of the soul.

Don was wondering about the woman he was seeing. Several problems in the relationship were rooted in traumatic experiences both had had, but they were working out those problems. All was well. We talked for a while. The conversation changed when I asked: "Why do you need this relationship so badly? Is it holy love or is it a hunger in your soul that she will never fill?"

Open-ended questions provide opportunities to listen to the movement of the soul. Good listening does not merely pay attention to what a person says. Rather, it probes to understand the heart and soul of the one to whom we are listening.

When we listen with an ear to the work of the Spirit, we hear God-sized questions. Here is a list provided by Stephen's Ministries:

- *Identity:* Who am I? Who should I be?

- *Self-esteem:* Am I lovable? Can I really like the person I am?

- *Meaning:* Why am I alive? Is there a reason for me to go on living?

- *Hope vs. despair:* How can I face the future with hope and not dread?

- *Reason for evil:* Why is there evil in my life? In the world?

- *Failure:* What if I fail? How could I live with myself?

Exercise: Imagine what a conversational room looks like. What size is it? What furniture would you find in it? What does it smell like? Where would you be sitting/standing? What would you be drinking or eating? Imagine yourself in a conversation with God. Where would you be? What smells would be present? How bright are the lights?

23

Exercise: In the next week, record some God-sized questions you hear.

- *Loneliness:* Am I really all alone in the world? What can I do about this aching loneliness I feel?

- *Addictions:* Is there any way to get out of this trap of addiction/compulsion I'm in? How can I stop acting in self-destructive ways?

- *Guilt:* How can I deal with the guilt I feel over what I've done?

- *Aging:* Why do I get old?

- *Purpose:* What am I going to do with my life?

- *Dissatisfaction:* Why doesn't my success bring me satisfaction?

- *Forgiveness:* How can I forgive people who have hurt me? How can I find forgiveness for the hurts I have caused?

- *Suffering:* Why must I, or people I love, suffer?

- *Broken relationships:* Why do I fight with people I love?

- *Regrets:* Why do I do things I later regret?

- *Self-doubts:* How can I handle the responsibilities I've been given?

- *Death:* Why do I, or the people I love, have to die?

— From *The Caring Evangelism Course* available from Stephen Ministries, 8016 Dale, St. Louis, MO 63117. ©1992. Used by permission.

Listening for such questions allows us to focus on issues vital to a person's relationship with God. We are looking for the story of God's presence. How is God's redeeming power made real in this person's life? How has and is the Spirit leading? These questions involve movements of the heart. And it is not just our immediate answer to these questions that counts. Instead, when we seek to hear God responding to the yearning heart, and then hear God's voice, we experience a wonderful moment of grace.

Listening is the means by which the door of the human heart is opened to the voice of God. Developing this gift is essential to the task God gives spiritual guides.

Chapter 5

The Gift of Discernment

The voice of God has many competitors. Some are loud and obnoxious; these we recognize quickly. Others are subtle; they play with our desires and fears with great skill and are discovered only through diligent examination.

To lead others to hear the voice of God requires discernment. We must learn to distinguish weeds from wheat, the kernel from the chaff. In the marketplace of values and with our television screens promoting alternate views, we need understanding and insight to know what is right, holy, and pleasing in the eyes of God. With the variety of opportunities before us, it takes discernment to know what is godly and will help build the kingdom. Therefore, we seek to develop the gift of discernment.

Exercise: Watch the television for one hour. How many non-Christian values were suggested or promoted during this time?

In the Christian tradition, discernment is always rooted in Scripture. There is no substitute for knowing Scripture.

> *All Scripture is God-breathed and is useful for teaching, rebuking, correcting and training in righteousness, so that the man of God may be thoroughly equipped for every good work.* 2 Timothy 3:16-17

The city and the church in which Timothy ministered were in spiritual turmoil. Paul, in seeking to guide Timothy through the upheavals, declared that Timothy ought not run after every wind that blows, but should instead stick with the sure, God-breathed gospel words of Scripture. Through these words, we get a deeper sense of the voice of God.

Discernment requires not only deep listening to the voice of God but also hearing that voice in the context of life. Life is a messy affair. Sin and its consequences are always present. Our desires and fears play games with our ears. What we should hear, we ignore. What we should resist attracts our attention. Knowing that evil masks itself as good, a spiritual guide listens carefully to the background noise of everyday life.

When David came to visit me, he wanted to talk about the direction of the church. The routines of church life no longer seemed to touch his soul. My preaching was boring. The members of the church seemed preoccupied with the weather, the mundane idiosyncrasies of people, and family. There was not enough outreach. He was dissatisfied. He wanted to talk about revitalizing the church.

No doubt he spoke truth. I'm sure my sermons could use improvement. The church could use some revival. But his words needed more fleshing out. The dissatisfaction of his soul could not be satisfied with a new church program or a revival of the church. David needed to experience the consolation of Christ. To help David, I needed to hear the background noise of his life.

His life has a context. Like all of us, he was born with a genetic inheritance into a family that lived in a community that was part of a nation. As he grew, he went to schools where he met teachers and peers. After graduation he went to work with those coming from other communities of faith and possessing different values. David's spiritual growth had taken place in the context of his life, where the brokenness of humanity and the grace of Christ intersect. Being a spiritual guide in David's life required attention to the context of his life.

Exercise: Read John 4. Did Jesus speak words of judgment? How did the knowledge of the Samaritan woman's past help Jesus guide her to the truth?

An Inheritance

All of us come into the world with blessings and curses that affect us all our lives. Consider the following list:

- gender
- appearance
- disabilities—learning, mental, and physical
- abilities
- personality
- family
- birthdate, birthplace
- genetic medical conditions (e.g., a family history of heart disease, breast cancer, depression)
- fetal alcohol syndrome, HIV infection, and other conditions of prenatal development
- original sin (desires of the flesh)

What inherited condition do you have? How has this been positive for you? How has it caused problems? What strategies help you cope with the limitations you experience?

As we enter the world, we do not arrive with a clean slate. Some factors we observe immediately; others emerge over time. No matter when we observe them, they are given to us at our birth, and their effects emerge as we mature. They contain the limitations and the possibilities of our lives within which our spirituality develops. Because of these differences, we express our faith in different ways.

Although I always knew this, I learned it in a fresh way when I met John. In preparation for profession of faith, I asked him to read a chapter of the Bible and answer a series of questions. By the third session, John had yet to do any of the assigned work. That day, I learned that he had a learning disability (attention deficit hyperactivity disorder) that made concentrating difficult. In addition, reading had always been difficult for him. Listening to John, I sensed his frustration because of his limitations. Listening to him, I started to focus on his abilities. His spirituality would take a different turn than mine.

Life Cycle

The current stage in our life cycle provides us with clues to the struggles and providential care we experience. Consider the following list:

- teenager/young adult/middle-aged/senior
- single/married/widowed/divorced
- children/child-free
- employed/unemployed

As we age, we move through different stages and cycles of life. Each has its own concerns and possibilities.

Joyce was a middle-aged woman whose youngest child had recently entered high school. Her life was changing. This experience was both frightening and filled with opportunity. In four years, at not quite fifty years of age, she would be spending her time in new ways. She was energetic and gifted. She and her husband Anthony sensed this would give them a chance to do new things. But Joyce wondered how she should use her time. Should she continue to work full time? Perhaps she could fulfill a dream to become a counselor. Her experience of God's presence was filled with these changes

Exercise: How has your church treated people who are divorced? Single? Unemployed? Elderly? How has this treatment affected the spirituality of these people?

taking place in her life. They touched her soul. Her identity was changing. She expressed fears triggered by no longer having her children within the safety of an arm's reach. If she went back to school, finances would be tight. Where was God leading? How was God dealing with her fears?

Unfinished Business

After birth, we quickly pick up innumerable experiences, some of which leave us with legacies of pain. Consider the following list:

- abuse by a parent
- abuse by one in authority over us
- rape
- peer abuse in school
- natural disasters
- accidents
- survival of a concentration camp experience
- death of a person close to us
- academic failure
- marriage failure

Exercise: Recall a traumatic experience. How does it continue to affect you? What strategies do you use to deal with its legacy?

Healing always takes time, and it often takes therapy. Even then, some scars remain for a lifetime. And each experience has a profound effect on our relationship with God.

David, whom we met earlier in this chapter, had been abused by his father. He had never gone to therapy. Now the pain of the earlier abuse was reemerging. Complex emotions were coming out. He desperately wanted approval. He was afraid of his own anger with his children. In his heart he knew he needed some healing, though he never expressed this plainly. He wanted the church to respond to his need. It was an insatiable quest. Changes in the church were never quite enough because they never satisfied his deep need. Eventually, he left for another denomination.

Cultural/National Setting

We live within a culture and a nation. Laws, mass media, divergent ideas, and neighbors influence the way we live with the Lord.

Consider the following influences:

- justice and injustice
- sexuality in mass media
- possessions (a blessing or curse?)
- religion in the public square
- discrimination

We can want certain experiences and resist certain callings because of our cultural experience. We face certain struggles and suffering because of our laws and political leadership. All these experiences help and hinder our experience of God.

Sandra, a twenty-eight-year-old woman, came into my office with a story to tell. At work, she had just learned that her salary was lower than that of her male colleagues. It seemed like a clear case of discrimination. She was angry, and her anger spilled over into the church's life. "Women are always put down," she said. "Men just like power and control." She spoke some truth. Discrimination is real, both inside and outside the church. Her anger had some justification, but it was turning her against God.

Exercise: Read 1 Samuel 8. How did the desire to be like the other nations lead the people away from God? How was God present to the people through this experience?

Discerning the Way

When we listen to a person's background noise, we seek to discern the way of God in the midst of that person's life. Acting kindly can mean something quite different to Sandra than to David. Dealing with anger meant different things for them too. The limitations that John struggled with were not only a source of self-deprecation; they were vital for understanding how John could grow in faith. The fears Joyce expressed had to be understood in the context of her new situation, which filled her with creative energy. Finding God's way is always a contextual process.

Consider a current television sitcom. What values and desires are expressed on this program? Do we see similar expressions in our lives?

The background noise helps us discern two vital concerns. First, we discern the prior causes that disturb the heart. What makes a decision a right decision? David moved to another church and experienced an immediate sense of peace. He took this as a sign from God. But a few years later he moved off to yet another church because he failed to deal with the root causes of his disturbed heart. By discerning prior causes, we discover more clearly where God is leading.

Second, the background noise suggests limitations within which a person must develop spirituality. John was limited by a disability. Another person may be limited by the lingering effects of trauma. By facing these limitations, we can discern how God chooses to be present in another's life.

Discernment is a vital gift as we seek to hear the voice of God bringing healing and renewal in the life of the community and the individual.

Chapter 6
Paying Attention to God

Growing as a Christian requires paying attention to God.

This truth is so obvious it is almost trite to repeat it. Yet no one who has journeyed with God for even a little while will fail to observe our tendency to ignore God. In days of busy activity, routine prayers and devotions—if they are observed at all—simply pass through our souls without touching a single thought or emotion along the way. We attend church services where the words of forgiveness mean nothing and the words of Scripture never stir our hearts. All this takes place even though we believe with all our hearts that Christian growth can only take place if we pay attention to God.

Inattention to God

As I write this my wife is preparing a seminar on attention deficit disorder (ADD), a learning disability. People with ADD have symptoms such as trouble paying attention, listening carefully, and organizing and following through on tasks, and they may be easily distracted or forgetful.

It strikes me that we are often learning disabled when it comes to spiritual growth: we have difficulty sustaining attention on Jesus. We often do not listen well to what is said; when we receive instructions, we fail to follow through; we are easily distracted; we avoid details; and we are careless. In other words, our behavior tells us that we find it difficult to give our full attention to God.

This is not surprising. We are fighting our own human desires, the world we live in, and the devil, who will do all in his power to make us inattentive. But to recognize these behaviors is not to excuse them. It merely points out that paying attention to God does not happen simply because we believe doing so is important. Paying attention requires diligent effort.

Exercise: List some ways in which you notice acts of inattention in your life.

After listening to several church leaders remind me that prayer is an essential task of ministry, I made a commitment: I would spend at least two hours a week praying for the congregation. That would be a reasonable expectation. That same week I discovered how easy it was to break my commitment. The telephone interrupted my prayer time. Instead of remembering to pray to Jesus, I started to think through issues. Instead of listening to God, I wanted to tell God how things ought to be. Urgent matters took priority. After two short weeks, I forgot the commitment. Two weeks later, I remembered. Then guilt took over. What was I to do?

Developing Strategies for Paying Attention

We live in the face of this tension: it is vital to our spiritual health that we pay attention, yet inattention frequently invades our lifestyle. To use the language of Paul, that which we do not want to do, we do. Therefore, we must develop strategies for paying attention.

Strategies fall into different categories:

- place and atmosphere
- order and activity
- accountability
- preparation for the next planned time

Exercise: In what place do you feel closest to God? In which place do you feel most distant?

In each instance, we ask the question: What helps us pay attention in a sustained manner?

Place and atmosphere

I entered the sanctuary. No one else was in the building. The light was dim. The symbols of worship—the cross, communion table, baptismal font, an Easter banner—immediately drew my attention. I sat down remembering the faces of those who sat in these pews. I found it easy to pray for the members of the congregation.

Later, I entered my study. Papers were scattered over my desk. Partly read books were stacked together. A to-do list occupied space in front of my computer. Though it was quiet, it was a workplace. My attention continually drifted from prayer to the unfinished work around me.

To help us sustain attention on God, we create a sacred space. It is the place to which we return again and again to pray. The very fact that we return to this place creates an association between space and prayer. It is a place with minimal distractions. Perhaps there are symbols of our faith within view: an open Bible in our hands, a Bible text on the wall, a painting or banner before us. The visual atmosphere helps stimulate our heart to focus on the Lord. Place and atmosphere help us sustain attention.

Order and activity

At one point during my teenage years, I learned to pray using ACTS. ACTS is the acronym for Adoration, Confession, Thanksgiving, and Supplication. I was taught that every prayer ought to include these elements. ACTS was a strategy that guided my thoughts.

Exercise: What activities do you do? In what order? How do you pay attention to God in a meeting? At work?

To sustain attention, we must develop routines that guide our hearts and minds. In later chapters we will focus on how to develop good and healthy routines in the Christian life. Sustaining attention requires some habits that force our distracted minds to notice the work of God in our lives. By making confession a habit of prayer, we examine our lives for particular sins. By making thanksgiving a habit of prayer, we look for what good gifts God gives us today. By making adoration a normal part of prayer, the eyes of our hearts see God more clearly. There are other routines too. Each routine is a strategy for helping the heart pay attention to our Lord and our God.

Who helps you keep on track? How do they do this? How can your critics help you?

Accountability

The book report was due Thursday. One page, double-spaced. Obviously the teacher did not intend that I take a great deal of time writing the report. She wanted me to read the book by a certain date. Simply giving me a date by which I needed to produce an account in writing helped me focus my attention on the project.

To help us focus our attention on God—to sustain attention, develop healthy routines, and ask the right questions—we develop relationships of accountability. Prayer groups, spiritual directors, Bible studies, and other relationships are useful in helping us sustain attention. Frequently, good intentions founder in short order. Discussing our spiritual lives with a group or an individual is often the stimulus we need to continue.

Preparation for the next planned time

A little bit of planning is a good habit. What am I going to do next time? Where will I do it? When will I do it? It could be simple. Tomorrow night at this time in this place I will continue where I left off today and pray as I did today. It could be more difficult: tomorrow may be a long tiring day of meetings with hardly a break.

Planning makes this habit of attending to God intentional. It doesn't just happen when there is time or if I am in my normal routine. It happens because I choose to make paying attention to God a habit in my life. Spiritual guides help people find a strategy that works. This is not an exact science. The various traditions are good but need to be adapted to persons and circumstances. There is experimentation as a person seeks a personal practice. The way the traditions are used changes over time as circumstances and need demand. A young stay-at-home mother with three young children will have a different practice than does a young working mother. Both will have a different way of paying attention to God than does a middle-aged working woman whose children have left the home. A single woman may develop a still different habit. One is not necessarily better than another. We simply want to find what works best for a particular person at a particular time.

In developing the gifts for spiritual direction, we learn how to pay attention to God in a sustained way. If we wish to listen to God speaking to us and receive instruction through the Word and Spirit, this habit of attention must be cultivated. Spiritual guides help others develop healthy habits of giving attention to God.

Part Two

The Practice of Guidance

Joe was elected into the office of elder for the first time. Having heard the words of the ordination form, he felt overwhelmed. His training had been haphazard at best. At the first meeting he was handed a church handbook and a church order booklet. The Chair welcomed him and gave a brief introduction to meeting etiquette.

After a few meetings he gained some confidence and began to participate in the dialogue. He understood the process of a meeting and what he needed to do to make worthwhile contributions.

Yet as he remembered the words of the ordination form, he knew that much of what he was called to do remained undone. What would he have to do to be a shepherd of souls? What goals for spiritual growth are legitimate? How would he find space in his calendar for this calling?

Joe faced his concern in his calling as an elder. Many people ask similar questions in other positions of leadership. Part of the responsibility of leadership involves mentoring others. The development of character and spiritual maturity is essential for the well-being of every person in every job in every church.

In Part Two, we look at key concerns in developing this ministry of guidance. These chapters are an invitation to form a style of ministry that makes guidance a vital component of the ministry of God's people.

Chapter 7
What Makes Guidance Work: Love

> If you see someone trying to get to heaven by his own will, grab him by his leg and pull him down again.
>
> —John Kolobos, "A Desert Father," in *Spirituality of Imperfection*

No method or program of ministry can in and of itself enable us to experience God's nearness. Too often we play the game of devotions or worship: If the music played at church were different, we would feel closer to God. If we read the psalms from another translation, we could hear God speaking. While there are times when music, a fresh translation, or some other change might be helpful, we cannot expect to experience a closer relationship with God simply by changing the programs and methods we use.

God's Love: The Winsome Embrace

In our relationship with God, divine love nurtures our growth. God loves us as we are: imperfect children who have a way of making a mess of things. We do not have to achieve certain grades in spirituality before God chooses to love us and be present with us. The whole gospel story tells us that our salvation is given us neither because of our achievement nor because we want it so badly. Salvation comes simply because God loves us. In love, Christ enters the world to die on a cross. In love, God chooses to extend the grace of Christ to us. God comes to visit us as we are and where we are. When God arrives, our house is not in order.

Exercise: Read Matthew 16:13-17:5. In what way is Peter imperfect? How does Jesus respond? Is Peter excluded from divine presence?

God chooses to spend the time and energy to clean up our mess and help us mature in faith. Our dirty laundry is cleaned up. Our house is put in order. But God does not stop there. Just as a parent loves her children so much that she does all in her power to help them grow up, God does not leave us where we are but helps us grow up. By God's grace we can be both free and at home with God. God's love draws us into growing spiritual maturity.

Read 1 John 3:11-18. Name some ways in which you experience God's love.

Incarnating Love

By incarnating divine love, spiritual guides can be part of God's work to bring families and individuals to more mature spirituality. By loving, their ears become God's ears. By loving, their words become vehicles for God's words. By loving, their actions demonstrate God's continuing acts of love. Such love cannot be faked. Yet without it our labors will be in vain. The godly love we show is a dynamic charisma for drawing people closer to God.

Exercise: Give some examples of caring relationships that helped people mature in their spiritual lives. Name three people who helped you on your journey of faith. How?

It started when Sam's parents expressed a deep concern for him. I visited him. Although he did not have many friends and indeed sometimes pushed people away, I liked Sam. But Sam had never made a profession of faith: "Too many hypocrites," he said. I ignored most of his remarks about the church, and we visited on a regular basis. For the first two years, he never came to church. Five years after we first began visiting, Sam professed his faith in Christ.

Reflecting on that experience and other similar ones leads me to realize the importance of loving relationships in the work of spiritual direction. We choose not just to do the work competently but to serve our sisters and brothers lovingly. The care they experience as we talk about our relationship to God draws them into a deeper fellowship with God.

Facing the Dangers

Speaking of love in the context of spiritual direction is dangerous because love is a much misunderstood word and experience. I know of too many instances in which pastors have abused their positions of authority and left people damaged.

We must face real dangers as we seek to incarnate God's love in our ministry. Here is a partial list:

1. Incarnating God's love has nothing to do with the warm feeling we associate with romantic love. Most, if not all, of us want to be loved and appreciated. Ministering to someone who expresses appreciation and love is intoxicating. The warm feeling can be a warning sign that the relationship is on the wrong

Recall some examples of love gone wrong. How did it damage the people involved? How did it affect the community?

38

track. Rather than building maturity, it may lead to permanent damage.

2. Incarnating God's love has nothing to do with creating unhealthy dependency. When we are making decisions for others or find ourselves being too involved with a person or family, we do well to ask ourselves if we have created an unhealthy relationship. Unhealthy dependency will not lead to spiritual growth.

3. Incarnating God's love is different from accepting everything another says. Confrontation is unpleasant. I prefer not to say, "You are wrong." Yet allowing sin to persist without comment will not lead to spiritual growth. Love is not avoidance under the guise of non-judgment.

Allowing love to enter the relationship of spiritual direction is vital to the helping relationship. Yet, as guides, we have a responsibility to be sensitive to the inherent dangers in such caring.

The Practice of Loving

In 1 Corinthians 13, Paul gives us a picture of love.

> *Love is patient, love is kind. It does not envy, it does not boast, it is not proud. It is not rude, it is not self-seeking, it is not easily angered, it keeps no record of wrongs. Love does not delight in evil but rejoices with the truth. It always protects, always trusts, always hopes, always perseveres.*

This biblical pattern for loving calls for deepening relationships between spiritual guides and those they serve. Some of the following practices are very helpful:

1. Be committed to the relationship. Spiritual struggles and concerns are sensitive matters of the heart. Only in committed relationships will people open up and accept guidance. Commitment is demonstrated when you keep appointments and remain consistently involved with a person over time.

2. Be encouraging. Many Christians feel they have failed God. They feel guilty about failures in Christian practice and ashamed of their ongoing struggles with sinful attitudes. Encouragement helps persons

Exercise: Write a note of encouragement to a member in your church.

experience God's forgiveness and provides hope for the future. Write notes of encouragement.

3. Recognize your limits. We are not all-wise, all-powerful, or all-loving. We, too, are learning to walk the road of faith.

Exercise: Who are some people you feel comfortable calling on for help as you minister? Do you consider them part of your team?

4. Listen. To discern and guide, we need to hear what lives in the heart of the person.

5. Focus on the key issues. There are many areas in which we can take steps toward maturity. But we cannot focus on everything at once. Discern the central issues and seek the Lord's will in these focused areas.

By loving, we establish a nurturing relationship with a person. Without love, our words will sound judgmental or demanding. Love takes our words and allows them to be caring and nurturing. The words pass through the door of the heart and nurture faith, hope, and love.

Chapter 8

What Makes Guidance Work: Seeking the Power of the Spirit

The Holy Spirit empowers our spirituality, our God-relatedness in all we do. We cannot make spiritual progress by ourselves, not even through our best efforts or strongest desires. Like Paul, we recognize that we do not do what we want to do. But—thanks be to God—we have victory through Jesus Christ. What we cannot do alone, Christ does through the Spirit.

One of the more effective programs for recovery today is Alcoholics Anonymous (AA). Participants in the program are committed to several principles, including these two:

- We admitted we were powerless over alcohol—that our lives had become unmanageable.

- We came to believe that a Power greater than ourselves could restore us to sanity.

While the alcoholic's battles are intensely personal, the way to recovery takes the alcoholic outside of himself or herself to a greater power. Victory, according to AA, does not come simply because of desire or hard work. Nor is sobriety maintained by desire or hard work. Help from a greater power is necessary.

Exercise: Read Genesis 4 and Romans 7. What does God reveal about the power of sin in Cain's life? In Paul's life? How do we escape this power? Can you provide a personal example?

Long before AA developed the Twelve-Step Program, the people of God acknowledged their hopeless captivity in sin and their need to turn to God for saving grace. The transformation of the Christian can take place only through the work of the Holy Spirit. Neither individuals who wish to grow in their spiritual lives nor their spiritual guides can make that growth happen by themselves.

Prayer and the Power of the Spirit

This simple truth makes prayer essential. We need God to work in us to will and to act. We need to receive strength from the Spirit. The Spirit takes the dry bones of our strategies and empowers them for the transformation of our lives.

A spiritual guide has a special role here. He or she prays for another person. Like Elijah praying repeatedly for rain, the spiritual guide prays repeatedly for the refreshing rain of God's Spirit to enter and empower another's life.

The importance of this ministry has come home to me again and again as I have ministered to people experiencing trauma in their lives.

Exercise: When has the prayer of others for you been especially significant in your life? In the life of someone close to you?

Joe's wife had recently passed away. While I visited with him, he confessed his inability to pray. It was as if his prayers bounced off the ceiling, and that was on the good days. Many days there were no words to use in prayer. He sat in silence and with increasing guilt. We spoke of his inner turmoil and how the groaning of his heart was itself a prayer to God. Yet his greatest comfort was this: that the prayers of God's people lifted him into the presence of God.

Evelyn experienced the trauma of a divorce. At one point she too confessed that she was finding prayer next to impossible. The routine prayers at the dinner table flowed off her lips without thought. Private prayers were nonexistent. I understood her struggle. Reminding her of the great importance of prayer and encouraging her to pray would only have emphasized her struggle. I recognized her struggle, yet knew that this was her journey. Healing would take time. In her silent struggle, I discovered the importance of my prayers for her and with her. What I could not do and what she could not do, the Spirit could do. The Spirit could lead her on her journey and bring healing into her life.

Trauma is not the only time in our lives when we need the prayers of brothers and sisters in Christ. The journey of faith is a journey of transformation. It is a process in which we are often forgetful.

Name three struggles in your own spiritual growth. Did you ask for the prayers of your family or friends? Why or why not?

Tom and Theresa pledged themselves to a regular devotional life with their children. They agreed that after supper each night, they would read a children's Bible with their children and have prayer time. The next time I visited them, they confessed their failures: the first week, they remembered three times; the fourth week, they remembered once.

In establishing new habits for Christian practice, the words of Paul ring true: what I want to do, I don't do; what I don't want to do, this I do. This is a struggle of the heart that we cannot fight alone. As individuals, we are often forgetful or we fail to take the struggle of our heart as seriously as we should.

The spiritual guide steps into the struggle with her or his own prayers of intercession. Recognizing that in our struggle we depend on the power of the Spirit to make change, we seek out God and ask for the Spirit's presence.

Committed to Prayer

In making this commitment to pray for others, we face a personal struggle. As I began my ministry, I learned to say, "I'll pray for you." After some years in ministry, this phrase made me feel very uncomfortable. I knew that I forgot my promise as often, if not more often, than I kept it. Then I heard how another pastor made the promise to pray: "When I think of you, I will pray for you." I embraced this approach as being much more honest, yet it still left me uncomfortable. How often did I think of Joe or Theresa or Evelyn? The commitment to prayer requires a practice of prayer.

Exercise: When you meet in group settings, what kinds of concerns do you pray for? Which concerns are generally excluded?

Here are some suggestions:

1. As you meet with other officebearers or spiritual directors, take time for prayer. It is important to be as specific as you are able to be in this time of prayer. Remember that an hour spent in prayer together is not wasted. Seeking the Spirit's presence and power is vital to the well-being of God's people.

2. Every Sunday before the service or during a quiet time in the service, pray for those in your care. In church we see many people for whom we are committed to pray. Their presence—or absence—is a reminder for prayer.

3. Before and after each visit, pray for those with whom you visit. The needs, concerns, and struggles of those whom we are visiting are very prominent in our thinking at that moment. Our prayers can be specific and meaningful.

Exercise: What improvements could you make to your commitment to pray for others?

4. When you think of them, pray for them. Prayer is always better than gossip. Who knows . . . perhaps this moment of remembering is the Spirit's reminder to pray.

5. Make it part of your personal prayer life. Our personal prayer lives vary, and we need to experience growth. By embracing certain people and their struggles in our prayers, we develop our prayer lives and bless those for whom we pray.

We are on a spiritual journey in which the Spirit empowers our lives and enables us to follow Christ. Our prayers for each other are an important part of our ministry.

Confidence in God

Our faithful God will respond to our prayers. Individuals will experience the embracing love of God and the enabling power of the Spirit. Spiritual growth will become evident.

Because there is no substitute for God's love for us or the Spirit's power working for us, there is no substitute for the love or prayer of a spiritual guide. Techniques cannot replace love. Wise words of advice cannot replace devoted prayer. But when the Holy Spirit and love are present, we can have confidence. Our work is not in vain.

Chapter 9
The Goals of Guidance

We need guidance at different moments in our lives. I am comfortable in my ministry now, but I know that someday the Lord may call me to another ministry. Last year, I felt an urgent need to deepen my experience of the Lord's presence in my life, so I sought people who could help me. Others have similar experiences. Depending on our particular needs, our goals for guidance change.

Exercise: If you were to ask Jesus one question about your life, what would that be? How would knowing the answer help you grow in your faith life?

There are three common reasons we seek spiritual direction: to feel closer to God, to deepen our sense of Christian identity, and to develop a sense of our calling. With the ambiguities of life, our reasons are seldom limited to only one concern. Yet establishing our primary concern assists us in developing a more focused strategy for growth.

Finding Home

The heart's true home is with God. To be at home is to be at ease, to be comfortable. Home is a place of shelter, a haven of love where we are valued and cared for. And at the center of our being, our hearts are inescapably connected to God, our home. We have our lives and our existence through God, and within his embrace we can relax and be loved. The heart is at home only when we celebrate and enjoy this connection with God.

When was the last time you felt "at home" with God? Describe that experience.

From Adam and Eve's walks with God in paradise to the new creation of Revelation 21, we discover that to be fully human we must be fully with God. Adam and Eve's fall into sin led to a deepening alienation from God. Through its descent into gloom, humanity learned that being away from God makes the heart cry out in despair and lose its way in the world. But in Christ, God chooses to meet us in our gloom. In Christ, God chooses to lift us out of our alienation and take us back home. Through Christ, we are once again given the name of daughter and son of the Most High. Jesus Christ takes us back home.

Paying attention to God lets us experience home. When I was a child going to school, our arrival home was always greeted with a cup of tea and a snack around the kitchen table. We shared the events of our day with each other. Mom listened, calmed our nerves, and sometimes gave some direction. Paying attention to God can be like that. It is a time of experiencing our homecoming. God listens, calms our nerves, and reconnects us to the central truths of our lives.

In Search of Identity

In this home where we are loved, we gain an identity. We were made in the image and likeness of God. We are re-created in the image of Christ, and he is fundamental to our identity.

Exercise: Name some Christian heroes. Why are they important to you? How can Jesus be a hero to you?

Imitation can be a way of learning. Sports heroes sell an image. My children want the shoes and clothes they wear. By imitating their heroes' styles and actions, they try to become like their heroes. They watch the moves of Wayne Gretzky, fully intending to try them the next time they play hockey.

Paying attention to God helps us imitate Christ. Our eyes turn to Jesus Christ and see a person who is compassionate and gracious, forgiving and patient, just and perfect, teaching, praying, and healing, confronting some and being gentle with others. By looking intently at Jesus, in whose image we are created, we gain a new self-image.

Looking for a Calling

Enjoying our place at home with God and having received a new self-image, we are called into service.

God is busy in this world. The dimensions of God's busyness are as great as the world itself. No place escapes his notice; no activity fails to attract his attention. In every place and action, God is busy. Even in clearly wicked activity, God is busy with judgment. And where judgment is, Christ announces that his death covers sin.

In a world where God works, we are pressed into service. This sense of calling has three sides. First, every Christian is called to act in a way compatible with the fruit of the Spirit (for example, an act of kindness toward a fellow employee). Second, every Christian is called to influence every area of his or her activity so that there is submission to the will of God (for example, a large company chooses to take an environmentally sensitive approach to waste disposal). Third, Christians may find that God leads them to a different area of work (for example, we create a new business in an impoverished area of the world).

Exercise: Read John 5:1-17. How was God "at work to this very day"? Where would you see God at work today? What does that mean for our working alongside God?

Bringing It Together

Discerning the primary concern is vital to effective spiritual guidance. As we listen, we pay attention to one question: How is God pulling this person toward the future our Lord is making? After all, what is most important is not so much what I want at this time in my life, but how God is leading. Discerning God's goal in the midst of our changing lives helps us grow in grace.

Chapter 10
The Process of Guidance

When our first child entered our lives, we wondered about her growth. Was it normal for her to sleep so much? What about her smile? When would she learn to turn over on her own? So we bought a book called *The First Twelve Months.* It gave us a month-by-month description of a baby's growth and development, discussed many of our concerns, and offered some helpful warnings. All of it helped us understand what to expect and what we could do to encourage our daughter's growth.

Exercise: List three activities you see maturing Christians doing.

Christian growth follows certain patterns too. When a person chooses to live with God, there is a consequence. God chooses to transform her life. Knowledge grows. Faith increases. The fruits of the Spirit become evident. For all the differences between people, there is a similarity in the work that the Spirit does in our lives.

A New Set of Clothes

Paul explains the process of transformation with the image of getting dressed and undressed. We take off the old nature and put on the new nature. The old nature is all that rebels against God and holiness. The new nature is the image of Christ. When we grow, we put aside all that does not fit with Christ and nurture all that does belong to Christ.

This image is helpful. What we wear projects an image to those who see us. Do we want to look efficient and neat? The clothing of a business executive will help. Do we want to look more studious? Perhaps a more crumpled professorial look will do. Do we want to look caring? Softer lines and pleasant colors. Do we want to be our own person? Something unique and a bit out of place will be perfect. An image is attached to our clothes, and with that image come certain behaviors. These stereotypes become part of the way we imagine ourselves and our world. Political leaders and television stars hire image consultants for this very reason.

What do your clothes say about you?

Putting Out the Garbage

The old clothes we wear, says Paul, are filled with sins. The following list is found in Scripture:

Put to death, therefore, whatever belongs to your earthly nature: sexual immorality, impurity, lust, evil desires and greed, which is idolatry. . .you must rid yourselves of all such things as these: anger, rage, malice, slander, and filthy language from your lips. Do not lie to each other, since you have taken off your old self with its practices. . . .

Colossians 3:5-9

In the history of the church, we have the list of seven deadly sins. The Heidelberg Catechism gives us a rundown as it explains the Ten Commandments, and other lists are available to further guide our thinking. These lists of sins are guides that help focus our attention. Recognizing that sin inevitably destroys, we begin to rid ourselves of such behaviors and attitudes.

The old clothes of sin must go if Christians wish to grow. Overcoming sin and sinful desire is a several-step process that is a fundamental part of the Christian life:

1. Identify the sin. How and when does it show up?

2. Pray for forgiveness and the Spirit's power to overcome sin.

3. Change your lifestyle so that the triggers of temptation are not as visible. For example, trips to the mall can encourage our desire for new things; restricting trips to the mall to those times when we have a particular need limits opportunities that encourage unhealthy desire.

4. Find others who will stand with you in your fight. Support groups and prayer groups can be helpful.

Getting All Dressed Up

As we shed our old clothes, we deliberately put on Christ. The following list from Paul is helpful:

Clothe yourselves with compassion, kindness, humility, gentleness, and patience. Bear with each other and forgive whatever grievances you may have

Exercise: Use five adjectives to describe yourself. To what extent do they reflect your vision of the Christian life?

Consider anger. Name three changes in behavior that could help a person deal with anger.

against one another. Forgive as the Lord forgave you.
And over all these virtues put on love. . . .

Colossians 3:12-14

Exercise: Consider patience.
What three activities could
help a person develop the
habit of patience?

These virtues are the likeness of Christ. Virtues are expressed in deeds. I do not forgive in general; I forgive this particular sin and this person. I grow in service by choosing to do particular deeds.

At first, choosing to do these particular deeds may seem artificial. The deeds themselves do not save us or even create growth. Yet they can be the occasions the Spirit uses to transform our hearts. By being deliberate in our good choices, we seek to promote the transformation of our lives.

As we put on these new Christlike clothes, the following steps may be helpful:

1. With prayer, identify an area for growth.

2. List some deeds associated with this area of growth. For example, generosity could be associated with deeds such as giving to the church, making an anonymous special gift to a certain person, or becoming involved with an anti-poverty mission. Loving your enemies could be associated with deeds such as inviting a person whom you dislike over for dinner.

3. Choose one or two particular deeds. Pray for the Spirit's renewing power to bless your activity and transform your life.

4. Find others who will help you keep your commitments. Support groups, prayer partners, and organized activities can help by providing some accountability.

Even Good Changes Are Difficult

The process is not difficult to understand, but it can be very difficult to carry out. The old clothes, however sinful, are familiar. We know how to act and react. The habits are ingrained in our living. Putting these to death involves a loss of the familiar. We wonder why we must change. Anger and irritability and sadness rise in our hearts—even when we know the change is for our own good. And making the change is difficult. Habits of life and body take time to change.

Exercise: Recall a time when you wished to change a habit. What made this change particularly difficult for you?

Establishing good habits is just as difficult. I know that exercising is good for me, but making it a habit in my life is more difficult. This past January I joined a fitness club when a special on membership fees coincided with a doctor's admonition. I soon learned that the club was able to offer its low rates for one simple reason: many who joined in the post-New Year's rush quit within six to eight weeks. Their resolutions faded. The habits of their lives crowded out their resolve to become healthier people.

Choosing to develop a good habit and become a more Christlike person is difficult too. It takes time, energy, and commitment. Receiving support and encouragement as we grow helps us overcome the resistance we will inevitably feel.

As we put off and put on, we lean on God's grace. Every night as we go to bed, we can receive forgiveness for all our failures. The guilt does not have to stick to us and weigh us down. Every morning the Spirit comes to provide new strength. The supply is endless, and God never gets tired of giving us our daily dose of renewing grace. While the transformation is not automatic, it is certain: God will do it.

Chapter 11
The Management of Opportunity

Most of us who have been called to be leaders in a community of faith are committed people. We have responsibilities to our families, we have jobs, and we work with volunteer organizations. We know how daily responsibilities and urgent demands frequently squeeze out of our agendas the important and life-nurturing responsibility of developing relationships with God.

Believing that God calls us to this responsibility, we must choose to create time and space for spiritual guidance. Our actions allow us to enjoy a "Sabbath" space for the soul where we can be refreshed in grace and receive the sense of direction and meaning so vital to our well-being. It is in this space that we can celebrate the forgiveness of our sins and the healing of our lives. To create space for such work is vital to the overall well-being of congregations and individuals.

Exercise: How often in this past week have you confessed to being "busy"? How does being busy influence your commitment to being a spiritual guide?

In our scheduled and demanding world, this means we must set aside time, make appointments with God, and refuse to allow other demands to interfere.

Making Time

We choose to make time in two distinct ways: first, by planning, and second, by throwing away our plan book.

There is no substitute for making plans and scheduling opportunities. Increasingly over the years of my ministry, I find that members of my congregation are on the move. When our elders or I attempt to arrange visits at the last moment, we discover that most members are unavailable. Previous commitments and precious family time crowd out such opportunities. And respecting people's busy lives means making arrangements that are mutually acceptable, and then keeping them.

In planning my work, I schedule time for the work of spiritual guidance. I suggest the same for the elders of the congregation. We determine how much time each month—evenings, afternoons, mornings—we can reasonably devote to the work of spiritual guidance and

As you look at your planner/calendar, do you find times at which you are most available for spiritual direction?

then block off that time in our planners or on our calendars. We make appointments.

Yet sometimes we throw away our planners and make space where there was none.

John came to my door to drop off a bulletin announcement. It was a busy time. According to the schedule, I had to take my material to the bulletin editor within the next hour, and soon Letty would be coming for a scheduled appointment. But as I stood at the door with John, he began to talk about his anxiety about the possibility of losing his job. It became clear to me that this was a moment when John was ready to pay attention in a fresh way to God's guidance and presence in his life. I faced a decision: Do I stick with my scheduled life or do I make time for this holy moment? I threw away the schedule and made apologies to the bulletin editor. Sometimes putting aside our scheduled lives is the only way we can make time.

Exercise: Recall a time when an unplanned meeting led to a meaningful discussion on spiritual matters.

Some People

In spite of the great number of people who cross our paths, God leads us to be spiritual guides in the lives of relatively few. This is no surprise. We all have limitations on our time, energy, insight, and relationships. It is not God's purpose to burn out leaders. God, who is mindful of our humanity, leads us in the direction of useful service in the kingdom.

People enter my life through different means. Because I'm a pastor, the members of the congregation automatically become part of my circle of attention. When I take my son to his soccer game, I meet the parents of the team. Occasionally these limited meetings lead to opportunities for more meaningful discussions. The circle of my relationships can include many people.

Name four persons with whom you could develop a relationship that would build faith.

To use our opportunities for spiritual guidance effectively, we prayerfully select a few people or families for meaningful attention. I believe that it is helpful to focus on three categories of individuals or families:

- those who are drifting in their spiritual lives and show signs of walking away from the community of faith

- those who are particularly open to growing as Christians at this time
- those who have the potential for or are beginning to show leadership qualities

Of the three, the first is most difficult.

Jack's work took him out of town frequently. He had few friends in the church and attended church services irregularly. When elders sought to make a visit, scheduling was always a problem. Although Jack was not rejecting the faith, it was clear that he paid little attention to his relationship with Christ. At a meeting of elders, mutual concern led Peter to make a special effort to befriend Jack. At times, Peter was discouraged. Jack canceled visits and failed to keep promises. Yet Peter continued the relationship because he believed with the elders that Jack was God's child. The difficulties were part of the calling.

The other two categories are easily neglected. They are not "problem" situations that need attention or squeaky wheels demanding attention. People who fall in these categories are faithful and involved, eager and seeking. If we wish to build the church of Christ and help people mature in faith, our time is well spent with these people.

Selecting people to guide can seem arbitrary and exclusive. Such dangers are inherent in making choices. There are two ways to minimize these obvious pitfalls:

- a prayerful process in which we seek the Spirit's guidance, and
- a collaborative process in which we test our thoughts with others

These processes help us pay closer attention to God's desire for individuals and the church Christ loves.

Group/Individual Attention

As a young adult, I was part of a Bible study. Every other week we sang, studied, and prayed together. This meeting was a significant part of my spiritual growth. Some of what we did could not be part of individual spiritual guidance. Our conversations about our shared struggles helped us pursue the things of God in common ways and

Exercise: Name two persons who you believe may be walking away from faith. What ministry could the church initiate to try to have an impact on the development of their faith?

What groups have been important in your faith life?

bound us together in our journey of faith. I received the guidance I needed in a group setting.

There are times when group settings are of great advantage:

Exercise: Which kinds of groups would you feel comfortable leading? Bible study? AA? Parents of teens? Prayer meeting?

- When we share a common task (for example, providing pastoral care), we can seek God's guidance together.

- When we share a common burden (for example, helping a recovering alcoholic or a survivor of abuse), we can benefit from mutual support.

- When we wish to honor God's will for the building of loving communities, small groups can be vital in discovering God's way for us.

- When we are at a similar stage of personal growth or struggle with similar issues (preparing guidance for new members or catechism classes), coming together can minimize time commitments and maximize the number of people involved.

By developing groups as needs and circumstances allow, we can include more people in activities that promote spiritual growth.

However, there are some instances when groups can be a hindrance to our journey of faith:

- Groups can become exclusive.

- Peer pressure may interfere with paying attention to God.

- An individual, for whatever reason, may not function well in a group setting.

- The concerns a person needs to address may be so personal that doing so in a group would be inappropriate.

Not everyone is best served in a group setting. As we manage the opportunities God gives for guidance, we need to weigh the advantages and disadvantages of individual and group settings.

Planned Conversation/
Planned Follow-Through

Planned conversation helps focus attention on the journey of faith. Planned follow-through develops accountability in the journey of faith.

Much time can be wasted waiting for an opportunity to begin a conversation. Sometimes this cannot be helped; wasting time together can be the way to develop trust. More often, opportunities are lost because of a lack of focus.

In planning conversations, I suggest the following prayerful considerations:

- What is this person's sense of calling?

- What are the person's strengths and weaknesses?

- Are there any particular stumbling blocks to spiritual growth?

- Is there any one concern that the Spirit nudges me to consider?

- Are there any particular struggles?

- Are there any passages that provide opportunity for such focused discussion?

- Has the person indicated how she/he experiences the leading of the Spirit?

Exercise: Write a planned visitation. (See Appendix 1 for examples.)

By following these kinds of questions, we begin to narrow our focus and develop a plan for conversation that can deepen our experience of the Lord's guidance in our lives.

Then we plan *follow-through*. We ask the question: What is it that I do to help this person continue to mature in the journey of faith? The answers vary from nothing at all to creating a persistent regular time together to stimulate and encourage a person on her or his journey of faith. Follow-up may be by mutual consent. Or we can choose to pay attention to a person quietly and to persistently show love and to open new doors along the way.

An Example of Faith

Committed people whose schedules are quickly filled need to manage the opportunities God provides for guiding people in their journeys of faith. At times, this approach seems too organized, and such management takes away from the very experience we wish for: a conversation that deepens our walk with God. Yet it is here, in the midst of life with all its demands, that we are challenged to undertake the spiritual journey. By managing opportunity, spiritual guides set an example for living the faith even when our responsibilities are many and urgent demands are made on our time.

Chapter 12

The Home Visit: Renewing a Valuable Tradition

The home visit (also known as the elder's visit and the family visit) was a significant tool for spiritual direction in the Reformed tradition. Elders would enter the homes of members of the congregation and speak with the families about living their faith. It was an opportunity to take the principles of the gospel and apply them in the particular situations of home life. When done well, home visits were a blessing to the community.

Exercise: What was your first encounter with home visits?

Although times have changed, the need for spiritual direction has not. We need to listen to the voice of God and live our faith. In helping people grow in faith, home visiting remains a helpful strategy. Such ministry is a positive way to build the spiritual health of a congregation.

Why Home Visiting?

Home is a special place. Our homes can give us a sense of place and belonging. Family pictures hanging on the wall tell stories of loved ones. The furniture and its arrangement reveal a sense of comfort and value. This is the place from which we leave and to which we return. At home, children build memories. At home, adults want the freedom to be themselves.

Read Luke 19:1-10. What experiences could let a person say, "Today salvation has come to this house!"

What happens in the home is vital to the well-being of congregations.

- On entering Bill and Catherine's home, anyone could see that it was a people place. The kids had the radio on. Homework was spread over the kitchen table. Some friends were over. Conversation spilled from one room into another.

- Casper's home—a house where he lived with a few friends—had the feel of temporary quarters. His friends were unsettled and on the move. Their place had little private space and personal touch.

- Peter's home was meticulous. Every plant was dusted and every object was in its proper place. Visitors were anxious about upsetting Peter's sense of order.

- Nel and Dick each had their own domain. The kitchen was her place. Dick's shop filled the garage.

Exercise: List a few ingredients of home life that are critical to the development of spirituality.

If families are the basic unit of a society, and if homes are special places in the lives of people, then what happens in the home is of critical importance to the spiritual welfare of the congregation. Is love being modeled? Do the parents seek to lead by their example? By entering the home, we can sense the dynamics of home life that give shape to a person's journey of faith.

Home visiting provides unique opportunities to build the spiritual life of the congregation.

What Home Visiting Is Not

Home visits are not church management tools. There is a great temptation to change the focus of a home visit to make it a feedback tool for church programs. Questions such as *What do you like and dislike about the church?* and *How can we serve your needs better?* turn worship services, the pastor's sermons, and new programs into the topics of discussion. While such feedback is useful, there are other and better means to get this information.

Home visits are not social calls. Frequently, elders do not know the members of the congregation well enough to have meaningful discussions on spirituality. To begin a relationship, we talk about the ordinary and superficial aspects of our lives. This is necessary. However, too frequently the relationship does not develop beyond this point. If we wish to make meaningful appointments, we must get beyond the social call.

Remembering some past home visits, what did you appreciate? What disturbed you?

Home visits are not focused on issues. In every age and place, issues rise to the surface and demand the attention of elders and members. In my years of ministry, I have confronted issues such as women in ecclesiastical office, the charismatic movement, changing worship styles, and the need for a church building program. Issues such as these easily become topics of discussion in visits. Although discussions of certain topics are necessary in church life, the home visit loses its central importance if it becomes another forum for such dialogue.

Home visits are not complaint sessions. Too often, visits become the annual list of criticisms the members wish to report to the council—with the expectation that something will be done about it. Elders should not allow visits to become safe places to criticize. For home visits to build the faith and life of God's people, it is important to keep the focus on the spirituality of those in the home.

Home visits are not counseling sessions. When problems exist in families, it is easy to shift attention to those concerns. But as important as those concerns are, we must recognize the limitations of our task and our abilities. Leave counseling to those with the wisdom and training for it. Elders can be supportive of that process. But for healing to take place, we must recognize the vital role of a family's spirituality. Supporting and encouraging this spirituality is an appropriate focus of attention.

Keeping the Focus on Spiritual Health

Home visiting is most useful when three basic questions are addressed:

- In what way does the structure of this home life build the faith journey of its members?

- How are faith, knowledge, fellowship, love, worship, and other habits of faith practiced in the home?

- Are there some particular underlying spiritual struggles in this home?

Structure

Every home has structure. There are times to get up and go to bed. There are times for conversation and times for work. Chores need to be done regularly. Some homes are very orderly. Others are more chaotic. Although God gives us room to organize our homes differently, all must share a single concern: How do we create the space and time for God in our regular routines?

Exercise: What are some ways we can create space for God in our homes?

In our home, we have dinnertime devotions. We often play Christian music. Catechism, Bible study, worship services, and youth group meetings form a regular part of our family schedule. These are times and spaces built into the structure of our lives.

In other families I have seen a devotion to service. Parents and children go to a nursing home to spend time with the lonely or serve at a soup kitchen for the city's poor. For the home to nurture our relationship with Christ, our regular routines must express the high priority we give to our relationship with God.

Everyday spirituality

The practice of godliness involves particular activities and attitudes. This goes beyond time and space. When we set aside time for growing in the knowledge of God, what do we do? Is it helping? Is there a better way? When we practice worship in our home, are we in fact worshiping? Is there another way? Is the soup kitchen the best place to serve? Perhaps another kind of service would suit our gifts and energy better. How do I teach my children the art of kindness and hospitality? As a single person, how do I practice hospitality toward families?

Exercise: What practices of parents encourage the faith of children?

Frequently, there are no easy answers. That should not concern us too much. Practices of faith nurture the spiritual journey and help all respond to God's call.

Facing particulars

At times, particular issues stand out in home life. They demand attention and can be critical to the well-being and spiritual growth of all the members of the family. Besides the obvious issues that require significant counseling, there are some that need attention because of the major effect they have on a person's journey of faith.

What issues stand in the way of your spiritual growth today?

At the Anderson home, the elder soon heard a murmur of complaint. Dad did not spend enough time with the children. It was not just his work. He worked long hours, but it was the many hours he spent on church business that bothered the children most. Choir, Bible study, cell group—and now the council was asking him to coordinate a program for children of divorced and separated parents. Were Dad's priorities right? Were all his involvements causing the children to feel resentment to the church? To God?

Susan became sick. The congregation was very supportive during her illness, and she was very grateful. Yet the sickness was changing her. She had been a committed and involved member of the church. But now, as she was returning to health, she knew she had to change her life's habits. How? She didn't know. How was God turning this to good?

In a home visit, we can spend time with these immediate and pressing concerns. Answers may be scarce. Yet the way we listen to God's voice together, affirm the priorities we have as God's people, and share our stories of faith allow us to nurture faith and encourage faithfulness on our spiritual journey.

The home visit is not the only strategy for developing spirituality within the congregation. Yet the connection between the spirituality of the home and the spirituality of the congregation is significant. To enter homes with a focus on spirituality allows leaders to have a positive effect on the congregation's life with God.

Exercise: Can you think of one time a home visit might be counterproductive?

Part Three

Everyday Spirituality: Steps on a Journey

Christians pray and worship, work and fellowship, give and serve. Paying attention to God and experiencing the transforming power of the Spirit requires the development of habits and practices that lend themselves to spiritual growth.

Historically, we have called them the disciplines of the Christian life. Prayer, meditation, confession, worship, Scripture reading, service, and giving are among those practices. While these practices are the result of a Christian commitment, they also lend encouragement on the Christian journey.

Yet it would be dangerous to focus only on the typical disciplines associated with Christian practice. If Jesus is Lord of all of our lives, then each part of our everyday existence needs to experience the transforming power of the Spirit. If Jesus leads us to deeper experiences of Christian living, then we must listen to the voice of God in the midst of our ordinary lives.

Every relationship needs routines and practices to sustain the relationship. To pay attention to my family, it is important for me to be at the supper table. Sometimes I tune out the conversation. Sometimes I talk too much. But the habit of being there and the practice of listening builds our family relationships. In our relationship to God, we develop habits and practices that will encourage our attentiveness to God. As in all relationships, these need regular renewal. It is my hope that the suggestions that follow are helpful.

In Part Three, some areas of typical concern are expressed. I hope that these will be of service as you develop your understanding of everyday spirituality.

Chapter 13
The Place of Scripture in the Developing Heart

It is less important to ask a Christian what he or she believes about the Bible than to inquire what he or she does with it.

—Leslie Newbigin

It's not easy to read the Bible. It's easier to read it wrong or not to read it at all. To read it the way it is written takes some coaching.

—Calvin Seerveld

Scripture has always had a central role in the life of the Christian community. Even before the Bible was in every home, there were traditions of public reading of Scripture and Bible storytelling.

Reading the Bible at the dinner table was part of my family's traditions. The reason was simple: Christian spirituality must be firmly rooted in the words of God.

The primary purpose for reading Scripture is to hear the voice of God. We hear his voice when we grasp the real meaning of what we read. The Bible is God's declaration of the life-giving message of salvation. In a miraculous way, the Spirit makes the words of an ancient text come alive today. We hear God leading us into obedience, providing comfort, and teaching us truth. Scripture leads us to sing praises to God and weep with the saints.

Exercise: What passages of Scripture do you most enjoy reading? Why? What portions of Scripture do you find difficult to read? Why?

Yet, sadly, opening the pages of the Bible does not guarantee that we hear the Word of God. All too often, as we come to the end of the reading, the words disappear from our minds and hearts. Nothing holds our attention. We face a dilemma. To grow in our life with Christ, it is important to hear God's voice. Yet many times God seems silent.

The Voice of God Silenced

Anthony called, requesting the use of the church and pastor for a marriage ceremony. Not wishing to miss an opportunity, I reached out to him. After some visits I suggested that he read the gospel of Luke. He never read it. He didn't even start. And his excuse was always the same: "Too busy." At one point in our conversations we talked about his school years. As I listened, I discovered his secret. Anthony was unable to read.

Susan always read the Bible. When I visited her, she showed me her well-worn personal Bible. I asked her what passage of Scripture made an impression on her these past weeks. There were none. Indeed she confessed that Bible reading was more a habit than a blessing: "It seems so familiar."

Exercise: What are the most common distractions you face when you read the Scripture?

Whenever Bob heard the story of the rich ruler (Luke 18:18-29), he would remind those around him that it was not a sin to be rich. He cited Job and Abraham as examples. He reacted quite differently than the disciples who wondered, "Who then can be saved?" By defending the possibility of being wealthy, Bob silenced God's voice calling for repentance.

We have difficulty hearing God's voice for a variety of reasons. All of our reasons for inattention and all the background factors of our spirituality influence our ability to hear. Sometimes we can discover the particular reasons for our deafness easily, as when Anthony revealed his struggle with reading. But often uncovering the problem is more difficult. By trial and error, we discover the approaches that help us hear God's voice.

As spiritual guides, we seek to help people through these difficulties so that they may experience the vital renewing power of the Word of God. Following are several possibilities for developing an ear that is attentive to the voice of God.

What Text?

Anthony may benefit from a taped version of the Bible. Susan may need a fresh translation or a paraphrased version to break through her habit and see the Bible through fresh eyes. Spiritual guides pay attention to the choice of text. We cannot assume that the version of the Bible being used is necessarily the best for the moment. Each translation and tape has its own particular mood and tint.

Recall a time when you switched to another translation or used a paraphrase. How did the change affect your listening?

Simply by suggesting alternate ways for the words to enter our minds, spiritual guides can break patterns of inattention and provide a means for renewed appreciation and attention to the text of God's Word. Often I find it very helpful to read another translation/paraphrase simply because it heightens my sense of attention. At times I wonder: Is this really what it says? At other times what was familiar becomes fresh. By suggesting a change in text, a spiritual guide attempts to break through the barriers to hearing the voice of God.

Because of Anthony's struggles with reading, his fiancee started to read the Scriptures with him and to him. Not only did this stimulate their discussions about spirituality, but Anthony became excited about the good news God had for him.

Reading with Others

Marjorie was new to the church, and she was warmly accepted into the life of the church. A newfound friend suggested she read the Bible. Later, as I visited Marjorie, she plied me with many questions: What is so important about David? Do we really need to give all we have to the poor? She struggled to understand.

Marjorie was new to the church. But many who have grown up within the church also struggle with understanding the Scriptures simply because they know too little. The Bible stories they have learned are disconnected. Principles of salvation are poorly understood. Whatever the reasons for this lack of knowledge, the voice of God is dulled. Spiritual guides can help by connecting stories and guiding understanding.

When I visit with individuals or couples, my chief work is to make connections. I try to take the various parts of the story and connect them to one another: How does God's promise of a son make its way from Abraham to David to Jesus? At other times I try to connect the words to the fundamental biblical truths: How does the story of the prodigal connect with the great scriptural truth of salvation by grace? And through it all, we ask the question: How do these words connect to the daily life we live? What is God saying to us?

This kind of learning together can also happen in a group Bible study. For years, my wife, Klaaske, was part of a Bible study group. It was a busy time in her life. Little children frequently demanded attention. Involvement in church and school took many hours of her time. But

Following are some translations, paraphrases, and story Bibles I have found useful:

For beginners who need to know the story: the story Bibles authored by Anne De Vries, Catherine Vos, or Westerhof/Hagan.

Translations: New International Version, Revised Standard Version, Jerusalem Bible, New English Bible.

Paraphrases: *Good News*, Kenneth Taylor's *Living Bible*, Eugene Peterson's *The Message*, Seerveld's *Take Hold of God and Pull, The Way.*

Exercise: Read the Scripture with a child (perhaps using a children's story Bible). How did reading with a child change your attention to the story?

Exercise: How has participation in a Bible study increased your attentiveness to God's voice?

the Bible study forced her to attend to the Scriptures in a regular and disciplined way. Along with other women, she could regularly ask, "What is God saying to us today?"

There is an advantage to reading the Scriptures together. The communal discipline can keep us attentive. The preparation for and involvement in the discussion forces us to reflect on and attend to a passage.

The input of others can also help us in a more indirect way. As many people in the community of faith have studied and reflected on the passages we are reading, we can benefit from their insights. We can consult a commentary, a Bible dictionary, or a Bible encyclopedia to increase our understanding of what the text means. We can consult a concordance to help us find other passages in the Bible that relate to what we are reading. By reading what others have written, we can reach beyond our own point of view and share their knowledge, wisdom, and insight.

Spiritual guides can encourage persons to read the Scripture in community with others.

Reading with Imagination

A child's mind is a rather open thing. Adults tend to restrict themselves. Every magician will tell you, "Don't let children too near or they will see through the trick." Adults have closed minds. They think they are watching everything. They aren't watching. They have a routine way of looking.

—Dillon, *Short-Term Counseling,* pp. 37-38

Reading Scripture for spiritual growth requires imaginative listening—that is, hearing things from another point of view. For instance, in the parable of the prodigal son, we use our imaginations to find our place in the story. We place ourselves in the shoes of the prodigal: How do we demand our inheritance? On what activities would we lose all our money? What would it mean for us to be destitute? Or we can imagine ourselves as the elder son, complaining because the minister attends to the down-and-outers more than to us. Or we can imagine ourselves as the parent who is welcoming the lost child back home and seeking to love the angry child at home. Placing our-

Read Luke 10:38-42. Imagine being welcomed by Martha. What does she look like? What smells are coming from the kitchen? How is Martha feeling? Listen to Mary. Where is she? What is she doing? What would Jesus say to you? What one thing is necessary?

selves in the text is an exercise of imagination. We hear the story differently when we take different points of view.

Over the course of time, different methods can be used to stimulate this imagination. A book of meditations or a book with some good questions can be helpful. I have found that certain authors stir my imagination. Some friends find that reading poetry helps. There is no set method for opening our imaginations, but a spiritual guide looks for a way to allow God's Word to come in fresh ways.

We need our imaginations to open our ears to hear the voice of God speaking to our situations today. Too often we box God into the habits of our thinking. To be able to hear God address us, we must break our habits and listen to the other voice announcing a fresh vision of life in Christ.

Spiritual guides look for ways to help others embrace the renewing power of the Spirit and the Word. This is seldom an easy task. But when a person gets excited about hearing God's voice and delights in the Word of life, the rewards are many.

Chapter 14
Christians in the Closet: Personal Prayer

Prayer is the art of conversation with God.

In this conversation we have one enormous advantage: God always listens. Through Christ, we have access to the ears of God. There are no right words, no right time of day, no necessary formula, no particular conversational skill we need to acquire before God pays attention. God loves to hear from us.

Yet in prayer we often do not experience intimacy with God. Our conversations lag. The words become routine. God does not respond immediately. We know there ought to be more to our prayer life, but we do not know the way.

Exercise: Read Luke 11:1-13. How does God treat our prayers? What is the basis of our confidence?

Breakdown in Communication

Prayer suffers from all the malfunctions we face in any communication.

Intimacy depends on our ability to be honest in our relationships. But we are often less than honest when we pray. We say what we think we should say, what we have always said. Our fears, anxieties, anger, and failures are all hidden from the conversation.

Intimacy depends on time. In our friendships and in our families we know that to be close to each other, we need to spend time together—to share and to enjoy each other's company. Yet frequently we give God only the time it takes us to say our piece.

Intimacy suffers during times of deep trauma. Many people who are suffering because a loved one has died or because of some other trauma in their lives have told me that they find it difficult to pray. Confusion, brokenness, anger, and sorrow mingle together, making it difficult to feel close to God. When overwhelmed with pain, intimacy with God suffers.

Do your prayers follow a typical pattern? What elements are typically included? What is typically excluded? What does your prayer say about your relationship with God?

Intimacy suffers when we do all the talking. If we do not spend time listening, we never get to know the other person. Yet in our prayer lives, many of us spend more time talking than listening.

As our lives change, our prayer life must change. As we grow, our prayer life must grow. Our prayers are expressions of what lives in our hearts. When our hearts are troubled, broken, or dulled, our prayers reflect our dis-ease.

Spiritual guides seek to uncover these movements and guide us into a renewed sense of intimacy with God.

Making Space

Space for God competes with space for all the other demands on our attention. Children, work, church, friends, fitness, and the dinner-time phone call from a local photographer seeking new business require us to take time and make decisions. God is not ignored as much as squeezed out of the daily routine. A dinner-table prayer and a bedtime thank-you are all we manage. Yet clearly, developing our relationship with God requires more.

There are two ways to develop that relationship: a dedicated time of devotion and a consistent awareness of God's presence.

A dedicated time of devotion
To cultivate relationships, we need dedicated time. It's important that I spend time with my wife. We don't need an hour every day. Sometimes, when we're busy, we can find dedicated time for each other only a few minutes a day, or on the weekend. The pressures of family, work, and church life can demand our full attention. But we know our relationship suffers if we allow external pressures to stand in the way of dedicated time for each other. We need time to renew our relationship and intimacy. We choose to spend time together.

This is no different for a relationship with God. We choose to spend time to renew and develop the relationship. During this dedicated time, we have to have reasonable expectations. Mountaintop experiences of intimacy with God may happen, but often the experience is less dramatic. Spending time cultivates the relationship.

Exercise: Recall a time when you felt especially close to God. Name a few characteristics of that time. How could you schedule your time to allow for more of these experiences?

A consistent awareness of God's presence

In cultivating our relationship with God, one-line prayers are useful. In all our relationships, our conversations are laced with one-liners: "Did you see that?" "Susan was sure excited today!" "I worry about Anthony." We do not have to say more. The words are understood in the context of all the words we have spoken.

One-line prayers are like that. In the car my mind wanders over the faces of many people. All I say is "Lord, help Anthony today," or "Thank you for Susan's enthusiasm," or simply "Thank you, Lord." Each phrase cultivates an awareness of the constant presence of our Lord in our lives.

Exercise: As you go through your day, repeat a simple prayer. For example, "My Jesus, I love you, I know I belong to you," or "Jesus, let your kingdom come," or "Thank you, Lord, for. . . ."

A Time of Self-Examination

Many times our relationship with God suffers because of the fears, anxieties, and burdens of our own hearts. If I am afraid of being loved, I fear the love of God. If I am afraid of being abandoned, I fear being abandoned by God. If I try to keep my sin secret, I fail to be honest with God. In our humanness, we all have issues and concerns that block intimacy with God and dull our conversations with him.

If we want to grow in prayer, we must allow the love of God to transform our lives and heal our souls. Although it seems silly to imagine ourselves resisting the love of God, we soon discover that all of us have such silliness in our hearts. We resist because of what lives in our heart—sin and brokenness.

Self-examination is the means to expose these concerns and develop our relationship with the Lord. Through his Word God makes us wonder about ourselves. Looking through the eyes of God, we learn about ourselves. Christ's love is big enough to let us see the worst of ourselves, and yet know that we are loved. Self-examination allows the intimacy to deepen over time.

Name a fear that regularly troubles you. Tell Jesus about it. How might Jesus respond?

Finding Words of Prayer

Part of the struggle of prayer is finding words. Our prayers, like our conversations, are dulled by the repetition of words and the ordinariness of our concerns. To some extent, there is no escape. How many different ways can we say "thank-you" for food? While we can make this an interesting exercise in language use, discovering a hundred words for "food" does little for our prayer life. Yet words are important. As we express ourselves—in part, through words—we build relationships.

One way we learn to find words to express what lives in our hearts is by praying the prayers of believers. Christians have a tradition of praying the psalms. By following the form of the psalm and using words inspired by the psalm, we allow the Spirit-inspired words of Scripture to teach us to express ourselves in prayer. In addition, books of prayers are useful aids in learning.

Exercise: Read Psalm 42. Reread it in a paraphrased version of the Bible. Pray the words of Psalm 42, adding your own experience.

Many Christians keep a daily journal to help them put words and order to ordinary experiences. These words are useful in our conversations with God. Prayer is not intended to lift us out of our daily experience. Our ordinary lives are the places where God works holiness. So we need to talk with God about them like we do with our friends. Holy intimacy with God happens over the kitchen table and leaning against the pickup truck. The words of private journals are words we can speak in prayer.

A Final Reminder

Our Lord Jesus will himself teach us how to pray. The Spirit will take whatever words we speak and bring them into holy intimacy with God. Spiritual guides help along the way by reminding, prodding, and encouraging.

Chapter 15
Drinking Deeply from the Well of Salvation: A Community in Worship

Worship services are a significant part of our community life. On Sunday morning the community gathers and centers its attention on the one who gives each person and community its life. In God we live, move, and have our being. In communal worship, the community renews its vitality as it praises, confesses, prays, listens, and dedicates itself to God.

Certain times of worship stand out in my memory. At a conference where hundreds gathered in friendship and with great enthusiasm, my heart drank deeply from the well of salvation. At a special celebration in our common life, my heart was lifted to bring praise to God. The music, the people, the message, and the single-minded devotion combined to heighten our worship and make the moment unforgettable. It was as if the heavens had opened and the rains of God's grace had splashed over us. These are the mountaintops of worship experience.

Exercise: What was the most memorable worship service you have ever attended? The most disappointing?

I have forgotten most services. These were not poor services. They were the gentle rains that refreshed my spirit and spurred my growth. I have forgotten them not because they were unimportant, but because they were less dramatic. Most of our worship happens in these ordinary services.

Most ordinary worship services are prone to grievances. As the community gathers, it reveals all its warts and secrets. The service itself has a usual form. The pastor may not have had adequate time to prepare. The Scripture reader may have had a serious argument with another member of the congregation. A just-separated member may be sitting front-row-center while her spouse sits in painful proximity. A letter may have been written to the council, and the members may be wondering how to respond. Melinda's children may be arguing as they enter the sanctuary. The organ may be too loud.

Ordinary worship happens in a community where ordinary people with all their irritating qualities and limitations come together to look toward heaven and renew their strength.

The question we face is simple: How can we as spiritual guides encourage a healthy spirituality of worship for our weekly gathering?

We Are Not As We Shall Be

We come to worship in the reality of our brokenness. The only one present who can claim perfection is Christ. God did not send Jesus to condemn the world but to save the world. Christ's presence proclaims a grace that forgives and renews. As broken and sinning people, we come to Christ to receive this forgiveness, to delight in the unconditional love of God, and to glorify him for it. In sharing God's love, we experience joy in worship.

Exercise: Recall the people who have sat with you in the pew these past Sundays. How are these people experiencing brokenness (sin and misery)? What word of God would be healing to them?

Ordinary worship is easy to criticize. After all, sinful, broken people are involved. Every Sunday, there is enough brokenness showing through to have reason to judge. There is enough sin present to criticize. Whether or not there is truth to these judgments, coming to worship harboring thoughts of criticism and judgment turns our attention away from God and the redeeming grace of Christ. Our eyes see what is inadequate and fail to see the movement of grace in our inadequate lives. As one elderly lady said: "It takes the blessing away."

Dealing with these critical attitudes is vital to developing a spirituality of worship as a community. Part of the struggle is learning to accept the reality of our brokenness and our limitations as a community. These acts of acceptance are a work of love.

Read Matthew 7:1-5. How can we apply these words to our experience with fellow worshipers?

Rachel was a member of the worship committee. She and other members of the committee worked hard to make these services times of worship and attentiveness to God. Yet the criticism wore her down. We talked about the people—their concerns, their fears, and their anxieties. Sometime later, she spoke about her changed attitude toward those who criticized the services with regularity and for whom good news was only a memory. What made the biggest difference, she said, was when she saw them with new eyes: these were broken people who criticized out of their brokenness. Like her, they needed to know the loving acceptance of God, who is full of grace.

Breaking the cycle of critical attitudes and turning our attention to God who loves all is vital to receiving the blessing of communal worship.

Turning our attention to God also means we remind ourselves that we do not come to worship just to consume and then critique. We come to bring glory to our great God. What matters is not just what we get out of a service but what we contribute to it. In our worship we focus on God, bringing him the best we can offer. It may not be much, and it may be lacking in many ways, but our loving God gladly receives the glory and honor we bring if we bring it from the heart. Wondrously, even through receiving our praises, God richly blesses us.

Worship Begins on Monday

A spirituality of worship begins not with the service on Sunday but with the Spirit's work on Monday. Too often we focus our minds on Sunday's presentation—on whether the pastor and worship leaders grabbed our attention. Certainly, most sermons could be enhanced, and often the elements of a specific worship service could be improved. But in an imperfect world, these possibilities will always be there, and making pastors and worship leaders responsible for our worship experience fails to recognize our personal responsibility for the act of worship.

Sunday's worship begins on Monday. Gratitude expressed Sunday begins with experiences of God's grace on Monday. Confession expressed Sunday begins with experiences of sinfulness on Monday. Listening to God's voice on Sunday is stimulated by attentiveness on Monday. And rededication on Sunday is built by dedication to God's service on Monday. The spirituality of worship is rooted in the ongoing life of worship. Helping people worship better on Sunday means helping people prepare all through the week.

When I was a child, we had a ritual at home. It began Saturday night. At supper, we prayed for the next day's service. Six children proceeded to take baths, from youngest to oldest. We polished our shoes. Sunday's soup

Exercise: How have you experienced God's grace today? Have you given God thanks for all these experiences?

Exercise: What music lifts your heart to God? How can you make this a more significant part of your daily routine?

sent an aroma through the house. There were rules about getting to bed on time. On Sunday morning, either the record player or the radio sang choral praise to God. Dad did the dishes. These were rituals. While in themselves these acts were not that significant, and while at times we as children complained, the rituals ushered in Sunday, announcing to our hearts that the worship service would soon begin.

Times have changed, but the need for preparation has not. To worship well requires a spirituality of worship that includes all the days of the week. Following are suggestions that some people have found to help deepen their experience of worship:

- playing worshipful music at home or in the car
- listening to inspirational tapes
- praying for worship leaders
- praying for an attitude of worship
- refusing to be part of discussions critical of worship
- spending time in devotions/prayer
- making sure you have enough time before worship to focus your mind on God's love for you

The preparation of our hearts is a responsibility we have as we come to worship. We listen better when we are prepared to listen. We praise God better when we have meditated on the wonders God has done. We give thanks better when we have experienced God's love throughout the week.

The Attitude of Gratitude

To worship, our eyes need to focus on God. Gratitude is the discipline we use to focus our eyes.

Our lives are lived in giftedness. Each day as we experience the routines of ordinary life, we take for granted the contributions of others to our lives. From electricity to food, from pleasant conversation to gentle presence, ordinary people going about their lives contribute to our well-being. Throughout the day, we receive gifts that make our lives richer, provide comfort in our struggles, and give us the joy that we know. No one can live a day on this earth without receiving the gifts of others.

In gratitude, we choose to no longer take these gifts for granted, but to delight in all we receive and recognize in them the gracious and saving presence of our God.

The simplest way to recognize these gifts is to make a list of them:

- What do we appreciate about our homes?

- How have people helped us on this day?

- How have we experienced the love and kindness of others on this day?

- How have we seen God's daily provision for our needs and desires?

- How have forgiveness and renewal been part of this day?

In each gift you receive, God is present. Giving praise and thanks to God for the many gifts we receive focuses our eyes on the One we worship.

Exercise: At dinner devotions, write a list for thanksgiving. Every day of the month, add at least one new item to the list.

Attention and Inattention

In worship, God addresses us. To hear the voice of God, we need to pay attention. All the strategies for minimizing inattention and maximizing attention are useful (see chapter 4).

In addition, it is useful to remind ourselves of the various voices with which God speaks. God comforts, admonishes, corrects, rejoices, gets angry, weeps, commands, calls, leads, and encourages.

Which words of Scripture do you have a hard time hearing? Why?

Francis came to church expecting God to get angry with him. As a child, he had heard the angry voice of his pastor declaring how sinful we are. It was considered good preaching by his parents. Now, as an adult, Francis had a hard time listening and believing that the gracious words of forgiveness spoken during the service of reconciliation were for him.

Nancy grew up in a faith in which it seemed all was acceptable. The gracious loving arms of God embraced her every Sunday. One Sunday, as the pastor expressed

God's anger toward sin, she responded with anger: How dare the pastor speak in such a way?

Francis and Nancy, like many of us, limited the voice of God to their particular preference. In the process, they failed to listen to God. In worship we pay attention to the God who speaks.

Tuning Our Hearts to God

The daily spirituality of worship allows us to experience the riches of weekly communal worship. Seldom will the weekly worship service manage to precisely pick up on the experiences of our heart. Instead, it is the spirituality of worship that tunes our hearts to God. Ready hearts hear and respond to God. Ready hearts lift communal worship to glorify God and find his grace as he nourishes and builds the soul.

Chapter 16
Living in Community:
The Spirituality of Fellowship

We live in the body of Christ, the church. Throughout history, the church has been a source of great blessing to the world. When the church is functioning well, members' gifts are used, people in need receive support, and the community is enriched.

Recently, the blessing of living in community came home to me in conversation with a casual acquaintance. She longed to be part of a community like ours in which spirituality is celebrated and faith-life is a topic of conversation.

Yet I know from personal experience that communities are filled with numerous attitudes that damage the fellowship. Here is a list:

Exercise: List some troubled relationships in the church. How do they affect church fellowship?

- jealousy

- envy

- anger

- bitterness

- persistent negativism

- power struggles

- marginalization of individuals

- family feuds

- popularity contests

- cliques

- selfishness

- abuse of power

- manipulative behavior

- sexually inappropriate behavior

- selfish use of money

As we examine the history of communities, we discover attitudes that have destroyed communities or left them limping. Among those marginalized in the church are those who have suffered the results of broken community.

God has called us into the body of Christ, the church. What does it mean for our own spirituality that God calls us to walk our journey in relationships with others? How do we live together so that the fellowship of believers may be a place of blessing and a sign of the kingdom coming? What spirituality must we as spiritual guides encourage so that we live as the body of Christ?

Cultivating Forgiveness

No one can live in community without forgiveness. Sinners who by the grace of God have become saints still sin. And whether it is intended or not, sin causes pain in the life of the community and its members.

Exercise: Give two examples of forgiveness in the life of the community. How did that forgiveness affect the community?

The sanctuary needed some renewal. The carpet showed some wear, and some veneer had chipped off the pulpit. Some people wanted to expand the dais to make room for the band and the choir. A recommendation came to council for a renovation. No one disagreed with the need for a renovation, yet an argument ensued: "We should never have bought that carpet!" "I never liked the color." "If the worship committee didn't rearrange the furniture so much, we would not have a problem today." Past offenses were once again dredged up.

Sin, grudges, and past hurts are part of the history of any community. Living in Christian fellowship involves choosing to forgive the past, to put away our natural inclination to hold grudges, and to renew our relationships based on our common commitment to Christ and the kingdom.

A spirituality for fellowship embraces the power of forgiveness to heal and renew.

Seeing Through the Eyes of Christ

Consider a person who has been judged by the community. Imagine Jesus looking at this person. What does Jesus see? How does Jesus feel? What does Jesus say?

Everyone in the community of faith is loved by God through Jesus Christ. This is what we believe. Yet every time we sit together as God's people we see other characteristics. Today I heard, overheard, and participated in discussions that included judgments about people based on race, sex, wealth, dress, popularity, annoying habits, psychological health, and views on issues in the church.

84

Sadly enough, this was an average day. As God's people, we slip very easily into conversations and attitudes that create walls of division in the church of Christ. Such judgments have the power to destroy. It takes a conscious effort to see people through the new eyes of the gospel.

Our question must be, "What does God see in this person?" We no longer allow these other considerations to hold power in our relationships. New eyes see people through Christ's eyes. As God's children, we all are

- loved by God
- imagebearers of the Most High
- worthy of care
- sinners who need forgiveness
- on a journey toward the new creation
- gifted by the Spirit

When we see a person through the eyes of God's love, we allow Christian community to become a redemptive power and community in our world.

A spirituality of fellowship encourages us to see people through loving, Christlike eyes.

The Attitude of Christ

Paul calls on the Philippians to look after not only our interests but also the interests of others. He urges us to embrace the attitude of Christ, who suffered the humiliation of the cross on his way to the throne.

A breakthrough came at a meeting when Susan asked the question, "What can I do to help you in your Christian growth?" The group had been discussing what its Wednesday morning meetings might accomplish. Peter had come hoping and expecting that it would lead to an in-depth Bible study and prayer support group. Many others did not want to go in that direction. As the meeting came toward a majority view, it became clear that Peter would be disappointed. Then Susan opened the door. By asking her question, she made it clear that, at the end of the meeting, Peter's interests needed to be addressed. Instead of creating separation, the group members were then able to seek ways to address everyone's needs.

Exercise: Consider a person in the church community you do not know well. What are his or her needs? How could you be considerate to him or her?

A spirituality of fellowship looks after the interests of all members of the community.

The Loving NO!

Certain behaviors destroy Christian fellowship. For the sake of building a community, these attitudes and actions need to be confronted. Some of these attitudes are listed at the beginning of this chapter.

Exercise: How easy is it for you to confront misbehavior? When has that approach helped you? When has it bothered you?

Simon complained about the action of the council. At a meeting of the congregation, he boldly said that many others felt the way he did and implied that a recent decrease in giving was directly related to this dissatisfaction. His speech not only heightened the tension of the meeting, it also conveyed a threat: Change your mind or I (we) will use our financial power to manipulate the council.

While Christians want to give each other room to express their views and even their passion, there are times when members of the congregation need to be told that they have done wrong. What Simon did was wrong. If allowed to continue, such threats would destroy the community. At times we need to say NO!

A spirituality of fellowship is willing to confront sin for the sake of building community.

The Call to Patience

Individuals and communities grow, develop, and change. Growth, development, and change are all processes that take time. There are times when all seems to come together in great expressions of unity, and there are times when differences in the congregation seem to divide. These occurrences are part of a living and changing community. Patience is the quality that allows individuals and communities the time to grow.

List three patient people. When did their patience serve them well?

Living Out the Gospel

Christian fellowship implies a spirituality that helps us live in community. Our ambition to live out the calling of the gospel leads us to embrace the love of God not only for ourselves but for others in the community of faith.

Chapter 17
Work As an Act of Piety

Every Sunday, John and Renata faithfully come to church. John, an electrician, spends most of his work-week installing equipment and wiring in new construction. He meets a variety of other tradespeople. He buys the needed materials, and at the end of a job he submits his bill. He needs to keep costs to a minimum, especially in a tough market with many competitors. A favorite expression of John's is "It's a dog-eat-dog world." Safety issues are constant concerns, too, especially since a friend recently lost some fingers on the job.

Exercise: Read Ecclesiastes 5:8-20. Which words ring true to your experience?

Renata, a mid-level manager in a large consulting firm, feels the pressure of clients and bosses. Often she feels caught in the middle. The company insists on reducing expenditures. Yet service to customers is essential. Renata feels added pressure at work because of the differing values of so many fellow employees, who speak of their weekend parties, their children, and their work in ways that make her feel uncomfortable. Both John and Renata faithfully come to church, but they wonder about some of the conflicts they feel: How does God want me to be Christian in the workplace? What does it mean to experience Christ in the workplace and be Christlike in a very secular environment?

A Spirituality of Work

In our work we hear the call to serve our Lord.

—*Our World Belongs to God,* art. 51

The life of faith frequently retreats into an environment in which being a Christian is a socially acceptable practice. Christian schools and churches are places where spirituality is valued, prayer is honored, and Scripture is read. For all our struggles with spirituality, these environments encourage us to hear the voice of God.

What gives you satisfaction in your daily work? What do you find most difficult?

Our work environment is different. The call of God in the workplace competes with the host of other demands on our time, our devotion, and our values. Employees focus attention on a service, product, or cost. Frequently, those with whom we work do not share our values. The context is not as friendly to matters of spirituality.

Yet the call of God reaches us in the workplace. The transformation of our lives by the grace of God touches the values, attitudes, and practices we embrace in our work. God spoke powerfully against all who had pious attitudes in religious practices and violated his call to embrace holiness in the workplace. Embracing a spirituality of work is vital to our spiritual health.

"As to the Lord. . ."

Accountability is part of every work situation. We serve employers. We have clients. Managers and customers judge our work. Companies measure customer satisfaction rates. Managers discuss job performance with employees. Yet the Christian does her work with the conviction that the primary person to whom she is accountable is God.

Exercise: Read Ephesians 6:5-9. How does our relationship with the Lord affect the way we do our work?

Knowing to whom we are accountable is both especially demanding and wonderfully freeing. God calls us to good work. Serving well is not just a way of getting ahead, making more money, or pleasing our boss. It means we are paying attention to God. Seeking the good of those around us or the company for which we work is not a matter of pleasing others or gaining approval. It is a way of finding our place in the kingdom of God. This attention to God frees us from the oppressive demands of the workplace. Commands and demands are relativized by the words of a generous God. Knowing whom we serve opens the door to spirituality at work.

Work Within the Bigger Picture

Finding value in our work can be difficult at times. Some work is clearly good. When we hear that the life of a young child has been saved by the speedy reaction of a paramedic, we applaud. He has done well. We immediately attach high value to his work. Yet much work fails to provide immediate connections to a greater good. Providing a client with a new computer program may or may not result in positive developments for that company. The results of our work may be ambiguous and may only be visible after time has passed.

To develop spirituality in the ambiguous environment of the workplace, three tools are helpful:

1. *We need to participate in a positive vision.* Vision connects our daily tasks to the bigger picture. John's work helps build homes and businesses. Doing it well contributes to the well-being of the community. Renata's work adds value to the work of her clients. Having a vision of the greater good helps us have a positive perspective on our contributions.

2. *Seeing our work as part of a bigger team also contributes to our sense of purpose.* Each member enables another. One way in which our work becomes meaningful is by empowering others in the team to do better work. We are servants who help others succeed.

3. *Our calling includes a call to be salt and light in our current situation.* Doing good brings grace into a world where stress, competition, pain, and greed often cast shadows.

Exercise: Does your place of employment have a vision statement? How does your work fit into the picture? How does your work contribute to the well-being of others?

Values in the Workplace

Christians choose to live by biblical values. For instance, we believe that each person created by God bears the image of God. That value guides our behavior in the workplace. As I sat having a quick lunch in a restaurant, I could not help but overhear the conversation of six men next to me. One made a coarse joke. Their server heard it, and I sensed that she felt degraded. Two men laughed. Three did not. One said under his breath, "No wonder he has marriage problems." Although I do not know the religious commitment of any of the men who were there, I do know that some honored women and the others did not. Christians honor other people as imagebearers of God. Showing respect builds people up and gives them room to mature as individuals.

Write of a list of values that you believe are important in your workplace. What needs work?

There are many other workplace values: respect for property (everything from stealing to copyright laws to the appropriate use of photocopiers) and fair treatment in business dealings. To develop a spirituality in the workplace, we apply our Christian values in our daily practice.

Grace in the Workplace

Exercise: How do kindness and forgiveness operate in your place of employment?

Where sin is present, grace has a special place. Christians are bearers of grace in the workplace. Forgiveness, kindness, and hope are healing and upbuilding attitudes. When Peter came to work, it was obvious that Sam was not his usual self. He was angry and frustrated. Several people had already felt his anger. Peter took Sam aside at coffee time, confronted him, and listened as Sam revealed the source of his anger—Sam had just learned that he was being transferred. As Peter listened, he opened the door to further conversation. He became an instrument of healing.

When disappointments overwhelm us, hope opens new doors. In a world that can diminish self-esteem, acts of kindness renew the soul. Where sin is evident, forgiveness enables us to renew those who are broken.

Transforming Culture

Work is a place where our faith and our broken world intersect in powerful ways. It is tempting to reserve our spirituality for our quiet times and communal church activities. This would be a sad mistake. In the workplace, our spirituality has opportunities to transform not only our souls but our culture.

Chapter 18

Service: The Act of Selflessness

To choose servanthood is to choose Christlikeness. Jesus, as he finished washing the feet of the disciples, said they would be blessed if they followed the pattern he established. Becoming a servant means choosing humility over honor and helping others over helping ourselves. Walking with Christ will inevitably lead to this road of service.

When Marilyn, a young teen, was asked to serve at church dinner, she refused. When asked about her reluctance, she explained that she didn't want to be with the people she would have to serve. They were not part of the "in crowd." There was no honor in such service.

Exercise: Read Philippians 2: 1-11. How do the interests of others influence your behavior?

Jimmy Carter, the former president of the United States, picks up a hammer to participate in building a home for a poor family. While the deed has certainly raised the profile of Habitat for Humanity, his act of service is part of his spirituality.

As we seek to develop our spirituality, we battle our desire for honor and self-service to embrace the way of humility and service to others.

It Starts with Being Helpful

The church held a big potluck dinner in the school gym. When the time came to clean up, Mary went to the kitchen to start the dishes. Four women and one man came to her assistance. The custodian and a few others decided to put away the tables and chairs. Most of the others just milled around.

Who are the people who serve as models of servanthood for you?

That dinner was not unusual. What happened that evening is what usually happened. Everyone was doing what they were in the habit of doing. Discussing this afterwards, no one seemed to know why this pattern had developed or why it had remained the same over the course of many years. A number of people simply said, "It's not my job."

Many parts of our lives have fallen into a routine. Who vacuums the house? Who cleans the kitchen floor? Who

Exercise: Who are the people in your church who are examples of helpfulness? How could you become more helpful?

mows the lawn? Who cleans the car? Other activities that need doing are frequently considered another person's responsibility simply because of habits.

One way of developing servanthood in our lives is by choosing to break these patterns and to become helpful. We simply ask ourselves one thing we could do to lighten another's burden. We choose to join in picking up chairs and cleaning the dishes.

Servants Let Others Take Charge

Being a servant means that others are our masters. This is especially important for those in leadership positions. Letting others lead honors them and allows us to walk the road of humility.

The issue of control is a major concern of our lives. As toddlers, we tell our parents, "I can do it myself." As teenagers, we declare, "Leave me alone. I can figure it out myself." Independence and control are significant values in our lives. Becoming a servant forces us to deal with these deeply-rooted feelings. We choose to let someone else tell us what to do. As they lead, we choose to follow without complaint. We are no longer in control.

In what ways do you submit to others at work? At home? At church? What feelings do you struggle with as you submit to others?

This choice forces us to deal with feelings that interfere with holy service. Pride, the desire to do things our way, manipulative behavior, and the tendency to build ourselves up by putting others down are exposed as we let others lead.

Instead, through our willing service, we build others up.

I noticed this one day when Andy, a mentally challenged person, was put in charge of cleaning up the chairs. He was told he could ask anyone to help. As we helped, following his instructions, there was joy on his face. Afterwards, as I talked with others Andy had chosen as his helpers, we admitted that to follow Andy, we had to fight a battle within ourselves. We thought that our way would be better or faster. But each of us put those feelings aside. And joy entered our hearts when we saw Andy's face.

It's not just Andy. When we seek to serve, and we let others take the lead, we bring joy into community.

Choosing to Do Good

Although developing a spirituality of servanthood begins with being helpful to those around us, it continues when we choose activities designed to do significant good to others at our own cost. Choosing to do good means that we rearrange our lives, and it is never easy.

When Adrian decided to invest his time in the neighborhood, he chose to help a youth soccer team. He loved playing soccer and felt that this was a way to help build a sense of community. Yet this commitment had consequences. Once a week, he would leave work and go straight to the field, so he missed suppertime with his family. Some Saturdays were taken up with tournaments. Last year he refused to take his team to a provincial tournament that included Sunday play. His commitment to do this particular good had already meant involving his family time. If he continued, it would mean sacrificing some Sunday worship. He wondered about the cost.

Adrian's dilemma is common for those who choose to do good. We make commitments that require sacrifice. Serving in church functions, volunteering in service projects, and caring for needy people takes energy, time, and money.

While we must weigh the cost, doing good is rooted in the call to follow Christ. Being transformed by the gospel requires that we seek the good of our neighbors and community for the sake of Christ. Our spiritual growth takes place along the route of service.

We live in a time when most congregations and communities have organizations dedicated to doing good for some cause. The talents needed to maintain these organizations are diverse. There are many opportunities. It is for us as individuals and church communities to choose the activities that best fit our abilities and circumstances.

We can also do good in a less organized way. Many in my congregation help neighbors and friends in special circumstances. At times of sickness or economic stress, they provide a bag of groceries or a meal. This way of doing good, especially when done anonymously, builds Christian character. When we do not receive accolades for our gift, our hearts develop a deeper sense of our Christlike calling. Praise—important as it is in our

Exercise: List some programs that serve to build community and help the needy. In which do you or could you participate?

Consider a person in need. In what ways could you serve that person?

lives— becomes secondary to our service. It becomes a way of life that builds on the foundation of our new life in Christ.

Finding Joy in Service

Exercise: Share a story of joy in service with another person.

Marilyn discovered a miracle in her life. She had experienced a particularly difficult time in her life. Much had gone painfully wrong. Her marriage had ended, and the divorce had created deep anger and resentment. But after some years, Marilyn began to experience joy. She had learned the forgiveness of God. Once again she was able to show compassion to those who hurt her.

The change began, she said, as she joined the Meals on Wheels team. This time she was not receiving ministry. She was giving of herself. That first taste of joyful service led her to a new challenge: helping victims of abuse at the local Women's Shelter. The stories she heard were painful and often brought her to tears. Yet her heart was filled with joy because she was helping. Not only did she know the love of God for herself, but she was now serving others. It gave her life new meaning. It allowed her to use her gifts. It was where God wanted her to serve.

Joy is a consequence of living with the Lord. In service, we work alongside a loving and gracious God, and we seek to let some of God's love shine into the universe. As we do, the joy of the Lord enters our hearts and lifts our spirits. Service is an avenue to joy.

Chapter 19

Stewardship: The Act of Covenant-Keeping

God gives us resources. I am privileged to have a home, two cars, finances, books, and clothes, among other things. I live in a nation of rich resources and many opportunities. The Lord has blessed me. But what I do with the resources I have depends on my spirituality.

One of the greatest battles in spirituality is waged over the resources we have. Greed and envy are prevailing attitudes of our culture. Buying things to compensate for spiritual malnourishment is a North American pastime. For spirituality to develop maturely, our hearts need to experience a transformation that develops a holy sense of stewardship in our lives.

Exercise: Read Malachi 3. How should tithing and almsgiving be part of our spirituality?

When Andrew got his first job, he experienced a new sense of freedom. For the first time, he received a paycheck regularly. He bought a car and rented his first apartment. The television, stereo, and microwave were soon to follow. By the end of the first year, he was reminded of his responsibilities to the church budget. He meant to put some money in the envelope, but he always seemed to forget. Now he started to feel the money crunch. His monthly obligations were rising.

Jim and Cathy recently moved to a large new house on several acres outside of town. They had done well financially. Their children had finished college. Now they had the freedom to move to this new home and to take trips to the places they had always dreamed of. But their consciences were troubled. All of their plans seemed so selfish. What would God have them do?

Susan liked to go to the local mall. She was a familiar sight at the Second Cup coffee shop. Before and after her morning coffee, she would browse through the shops. When I asked her why she did so, she confided that it was just something to fill her time. She hated television; shopping was her entertainment.

A growing spirituality develops a deep sense of stewardship.

A Matter of Covenant

We live in relationships. Every interaction we have is saturated with covenant promise and responsibility. Faithfulness and service are vital qualities of holy covenant living. This is critical in an age where many have a hard time making and keeping commitments.

Exercise: List several relationships in your life, including your relationship with creation. What commitments have you made in these relationships?

Not all relationships are those we have chosen. We are born into the world, into families and communities. We have not chosen these relationships, yet how we live in them is vital to our spiritual health. Other relationships we have chosen and sealed with promises—for example, marriage and our commitment to the church. Being faithful in these relationships and serving their best interests require that we use our resources well.

Stewardship understands the relationship between our daily use of the resources God gives us and the quality of the relationships we have. The more we seek to possess for ourselves, the more we close our hearts to others. The less we pay attention to the demands of covenantal relationships, the less we pay attention to the voice of God.

Examining our relationships in the light of God's call to love opens the door to the proper use of the gifts of God. We begin simply enough: To whom am I related? To what groups of people do I belong? What are my clear obligations and responsibilities? What have I promised to do?

A spirituality of stewardship embraces faithfulness in relationships.

A Matter of Taking Responsibility

Learning to budget is not just a matter of getting control of our finances; it is an act of faithfulness to our God and relationships. With a budget, we set priorities.

If you have not prepared a budget, now would be a good time. What surprises you? What does your budget say about your priorities?

Dave and Grace came to visit me for premarital counseling. They were preparing for their lives together in a new home. We spoke of their dreams. They were very ambitious: a large home, three children, and successful careers were all in the forecast. I applaud couples who dream. But when I asked how they planned to make their dreams come true, I became concerned. Credit cards had become useful tools for their consumer habits. They had no idea of how they spent money, or how the costs of the things they desired fit into their monthly budget. Their dreams took on a decidedly selfish character.

Preparing a budget is an expression of values we embrace. For example:

- How much money we spend on clothes is a choice: do we embrace our modern culture's preoccupation with image or choose to do with less?

- How much are we willing to give away: do we give what is left over or do we choose to give the tithe (or better)?

- Are we more concerned with our possessions or our relationships?

- Do we choose to live a simpler life than we can afford for the sake of the careful use of resources?

While we have to be careful about making universal rules, choosing to do value-based budgeting is clearly an exercise of taking our God-given fiscal responsibility seriously. It is a time for seeking first the kingdom.

A spirituality of stewardship encourages using values to budget our resources.

A Matter of Taking Care

One value that helps us seek the kingdom is our decision to take appropriate responsibility for our neighbors and our neighborhood. What the Lord has given us provides us with an opportunity to take care of people and the creation. Rather than choosing to please ourselves and exploit opportunities, we choose to spend ourselves "on behalf of the hungry and the needs of the oppressed" (Isa. 58:10). We choose to care for our environment. These choices involve decisions about the use of our time and money.

Jim and Cathy struggled because they wondered to what God called them. Both their time and their resources could be used in different ways: perhaps they should

Exercise: We use the phrase "taking care" in a variety of circumstances. We take care of business, of children, of our environment. How can taking care be a practice of our spiritual lives?

spend some of their vacation time working for a disaster-relief organization. Perhaps they ought to contribute significantly more to the work of the deacons. Maybe a smaller addition to their home would be more appropriate.

They wondered because they had values that tugged at their souls. God called them to be good stewards; God called them to attend to the needs of the poor. Paying attention to God was necessary for their growth.

A spirituality of stewardship embraces opportunities for taking care.

A Matter of Charity

In our culture, money and power are often intertwined: "He who pays the piper calls the tune." Yet for giving to be gracious, it must lose its connection to power. A gift remains a gift only when there are no strings attached. But when we let go of power, we lose our ability to control. Whoever receives the gift may do with it as she or he pleases. This is difficult for us as givers.

Exercise: How do you expend yourself on behalf of the poor?

Joel had made it his ambition to help several members of his community who were struggling. He would arrive at the local market at closing time and buy, at greatly reduced prices, whatever vegetables and fruit remained. At first, when he took his gift to the struggling families, it was greatly appreciated. Later, Joel's attitude and the attitudes of the recipients changed. Joel had started making suggestions and became irritated when the families failed to follow through on his advice. Why didn't you freeze the beans I brought you last week? Did you make the applesauce yet?

We would like to place conditions on the gift. And yet learning to be generous without demanding control and power is vital to spiritual health. In the act of giving, we struggle with ourselves: Can we give unconditionally? Can we be generous without being paternalistic?

The connection between power and stewardship also applies to receiving. When we are in need, receiving can be an intensely difficult thing to do. It hurts our pride. It extorts from us the confession that we are not self-sufficient, independent, or in control of our own resources.

But why should we be? The cells of a body all depend on each other. That is how it should be. We need to learn to share in both directions, so that as members of Christ's body we will not be independent, but interdependent. We must learn to take with a generous spirit, so that we in turn can give generously of the riches God grants us.

A spirituality of stewardship learns the art of true generosity.

A Matter of Gratitude

All giving is rooted in gratitude. We earn a salary when we work so many hours a week. At the end of the pay period, we receive our due reward. Gratitude, however, recognizes that we have received that which we do not deserve. God's continual care and saving grace far exceed anything we can earn.

Exercise: Who are thankful people in your community of faith? How do they show it?

The attitude of thanksgiving gets translated into acts of generosity and kindness.

Betty, a single mother with two children, went through a very difficult time during her divorce. Many times, friends and the church community stepped into her life to provide for the basic needs of her family. As her life became more settled, she became a generous giver. "I know how much it meant to me during my darkest moments," she said. "I just want to give a little relief and hope." Gratitude shaped her giving and life.

A spirituality of stewardship is a way of giving thanks to God and to our neighbors.

Stewardship is a place where spirituality confronts the spirits of our age. The struggle we have to clothe ourselves with holiness in this area transforms our lives and makes them more godly.

The Home Visit: Preparation and Guidelines

Home visitation is a traditional strategy for ministry. At its best, it is a tool that allows the officebearer to encourage spiritual development among members of the congregation. I prepared the following materials for the elders of my congregation to use as a guideline in making home visits.

Preparation for a Visit

What takes place within any visit depends in large part on the preparation that occurs before the visit. This involves both the elder and the people he is visiting. What follows is a list of questions to help prepare for such a visit.

1. How well do you know the person you will be seeing? What is your relationship to him or her? Will it change when you come to visit as an elder?

   - In order to establish a credible shepherding relationship with members, we must be acquainted with their story. Because the Lord has worked with a person longer than we have, we will be hard-pressed to help a person grow without knowing his or her prior story.

   - At times there is a change in the relationship between an elder and a person. Sharing a faith story may be a new activity for some people. If so, the change in relationship will have to be dealt with up front.

2. Are you aware of any particular stumbling blocks to spiritual growth? What are the person's particular strengths and weaknesses? What is the person's sense of calling? What background factors are useful in understanding this person's spirituality?

3. Could someone else be more helpful in guiding this person's spiritual growth?

4. How does a person relate to members of the community of faith? To friends outside the church? To the values of the culture?

5. What ministry or service is the person involved with?

6. Are there some activities that would spur this person to further growth or that would assist the person in particular growth?

   - The desire to get a person involved in ministry and in particular programs within the church ought not be your primary concern.

   - We should not limit members' service opportunities to church activities. Other service organizations also exist within the Christian community (e.g., working at a local food bank), and there are many opportunities to serve in the larger community (e.g., volunteering for the Red Cross) and the work community. Work outside the community of faith increases the witness, broadens the mind, and deepens our service to the Lord.

7. What does the person read? What courses does this person attend? How does he or she seek to mature in faith?

8. Does she or he have particular struggles?

9. What could the person do to prepare for this visit? Is there a Bible passage that could be studied? Are there some questions a person could answer beforehand?

The Visit

Before walking through the door, there are certain practices that are important.

1. *Prayer.* Although we may go prepared, the Spirit of God can lead in new directions. All activity that is of lasting value finds its power in the Spirit of God. In prayer we seek the Lord's blessing and presence in our time together.

2. *Review.* We need to remind ourselves about basic facts: names, children, special circumstances, and special circumstances of the visit.

3. *Place.* We come as servants of the Lord to do ministry in the name of Christ, to serve God's people to the praise of God's name. Our attitude should be the same as that of Christ Jesus. (See Philippians 2.)

The style of the visit depends on a variety of factors:

1. *The elder.* Each elder will be comfortable with different styles. Some will be more structured than others (beginning with prayer, reading Scripture, discussing particular subjects, ending with prayer). Each approach has its strengths and weaknesses. As servants we need to keep in mind what will best serve those we visit.

2. *The purpose.* A crisis visit is quite different from an annual checkup visit, which is quite different from a discipling visit.

Finally, we need to keep in mind that what can be accomplished in a single visit is limited. Neither minds nor lifestyles are likely to show dramatic changes. Our expectations ought to be realistic. Our goal is not so much immediate gains as long-term growth.

Follow-up

The success of any visit depends on follow-up. If we wish to encourage steady giving, we need not only gain a person's assent but regularly encourage and hold a person accountable for promises made. If we want to demonstrate support for a person in crisis, we have to say so—not only in word but by carrying through with more visits and expressions of concern. Follow-up is not just a nice thing to do, but an essential part of the task of an elder.

Sample Visit Plans

Checkup Visit: Guideline 1—Philippians 2:1-13

Approach: In this visit, the elder uses a Bible study to initiate a discussion of the spiritual health of a person. Prior to the visit, the elder requests that the person read this passage and explains that this will be the basis for some personal questions.

Step 1: Arrange for the visit (purpose, time, place, and length); request the reading of the passage.

Step 2: Greet each other. Remember, this is not a get-acquainted visit. Do not spend much time on saying hello (perhaps only 10 percent of the time allotted). Explain the procedure of the visit (the steps). Tell him or her that you will keep an issues sheet handy. An issues sheet is a way of recording matters that are off the current topic but to which you promise to return in this visit or the next.

Step 3: Begin with prayer. Read the passage together.

Step 4: Use the following questions:

- Open: Who in your household, family of origin, or work eats the last cookie? Cleans the toilet? Makes coffee? Tidies up? Fixes the photocopier?

- Dig: What was the problem in the early church? What motives are there for living in unity? What stands out about Jesus from this early hymn? (He did not count equality something to be grasped, he humbled himself, he became obedient.) What stories about Jesus reflect verses 3 and 4? What movement does this passage call us to take (not count equality, humble ourselves, be obedient)?

- Reflect: How would things change if you consistently applied this way of living in your home? In the church? At your work? How does the attitude of Jesus Christ differ from that of a doormat?

Step 5: Becoming Christlike (a mature Christian) requires that we make commitments to our growth. What commitments (one or two) can you make that would help you grow toward Christlikeness? What changes in behavior or attitude are necessary?

Step 6: What can I do to help you? What can the people of the church do?

Step 7: Return to the issues sheet. If you have time, you may discuss some of those matters. Ask if there are other matters to be discussed. Close in prayer.

Step 8: Write down follow-up matters and make another appointment if necessary.

Checkup Visit: Guideline 2—Luke 19:11-27

Approach: In this visit, the elder uses a Bible study to initiate a discussion of the spiritual health of a person. Prior to the visit the elder requests that the person read this passage, explaining that this will be the basis for some personal questions.

Step 1: Arrange for the visit (purpose, time, place, and length); request the reading of the passage.

Step 2: Greet each other. Remember, this is not a get-acquainted visit. Do not spend much time on saying hello (perhaps only 10 percent of the time allotted). Explain the procedure of the visit (the steps). Tell him or her that you will keep an issues sheet handy. An issues sheet is a way of recording matters that are off the current topic but to which you promise to return in this visit or the next.

Step 3: Begin with prayer. Read the passage together.

Step 4: Use the following questions:

- Open: Why do we say, "If you want the job done, give it to a busy person?" Give examples. Whom do you admire?

- Dig: Who is Jesus talking to? What does the man of noble birth ask of each person? How do people respond? Is the fear of the one person legitimate? What should the person have feared? Verse 26 reveals the economy of the kingdom. What is Jesus telling those who were waiting for the kingdom?

- Reflect: Where do you find yourself in this story? How do you see your life as a gift? What has God given you that you can share with others?

Step 5: Becoming Christlike (a mature Christian) requires that we make commitments to our growth. What commitments (one or two) can you make that would help you grow toward Christlikeness? What changes of behavior or attitude are necessary?

Step 6: What can I do to help you? What can the people of the church do?

Step 7: Return to the issues sheet. If you have time, you may discuss some of those matters. Ask if there are other matters to be discussed. Close in prayer.

Step 8: Write down follow-up matters and make another appointment if necessary.

Checkup Visit: Guideline 3—Review of the Year

Approach: In this visit, the elder takes as a starting point particular events in a person's life, seeking to discern how God has moved in the past and how the Lord is calling at the present time. Prior to the visit, the elder requests that the person prepare by thinking about three significant events of this past year.

Step 1: Arrange for the visit (purpose, time, place, and length); request the reading of the passage.

Step 2: Greet each other. Remember, this is not a get-acquainted visit. Do not spend much time on saying hello (perhaps only 10 percent of the time allotted). Explain the procedure of the visit (the steps). Tell him or her that you will keep an issues sheet handy. An issues sheet is a way of recording matters that are off the current topic but to which you promise to return in this visit or the next.

Step 3: Begin with prayer. List the three significant events. Ask the person to tell the story of the last one of the significant events.

Step 4: Questions to discuss:

- What fears and anxieties did you have?
- What caused you excitement?
- What did you learn about yourself?
- What suggested that God was absent or ignoring you?
- What spoke to you of God's presence?
- Where was your biggest struggle?
- How can you sense God leading you in these struggles?
- What are some of the attitudes that helped?
- How did you experience Christlikeness at this time?

Step 5: Bringing in the Scripture. If you were to choose a character from a story or parable in the Scripture, which one would you choose? Why? As we meet today, where do you sense God calling you?

Step 6: Becoming Christlike (a mature Christian) requires that we make commitments to our growth. What commitments (one or two) can you make that would help you listen to this word from the Lord? What changes in behavior or attitude are necessary?

Step 7: What can I do to help you? What can the people of the church do?

Step 8: Return to the issues sheet. If you have time, you may discuss some of those matters. Ask if there are other matters to be discussed. Close in prayer.

Step 9: Write down follow-up matters and make another appointment if necessary.

Family Visit: Guideline 1—For a Family with Young Children

Approach: In this visit the elder arranges to have the entire family together. The elder begins by reading together one of the latest stories the family has read from the children's Bible. Discussion focuses on what the children are learning.

Step 1: Arrange for the visit (purpose, time, place, length). Ask the family to prepare a list of ten items they believe are important for Christian living.

Step 2: Greet each other. Remember to greet each child by name. Make each child comfortable with you. (Take a candy or a small toy along if you want to.) Do not spend more than 10 percent of your time in getting comfortable. Explain the procedure of the visit. Tell them you will keep an issues sheet handy to allow you to record matters that require further reflection at the end of the visit or in another visit.

Step 3: Pray. Read the children's story Bible. First ask factual questions: Did they under-stand the story? You may find that you need to retell the story in your own words. Then ask reflective questions: I wonder what it would be like to be David? Finally, ask listening questions: What is God saying to us? If God were to sit in this room and join us in this conversation, what would he pay attention to and say to us?

Step 4: Read the list of ten items important for Christian living prepared beforehand by the family. If this has not been done, take the time to do so now. Look at the list. What's missing? How does the family seek to work this out in family life? Be very pragmatic. What exactly are they doing? If helping others is important, how do they help others?

Step 5: Making commitments is an important way of growing as a Christian. What commitments do they believe God is calling them toward at this time?

Step 6: How can I help you? How can the church help you in your Christian growth?

Step 7: Return to the issues sheet. If you have time, discuss some of these. Add others if necessary. If there are some matters yet to be discussed, arrange for a special meet-ing. Close in prayer.

Step 8: Write down follow-up items.

Family Visit: Guideline 2—For a Family with Teens

Approach: In this visit the elder arranges to have the entire family together. Discussion focuses on how the children (especially teens) are making personal commitments.

Step 1: Arrange for the visit (purpose, time, place, length).

Step 2: Greet each other. Remember to greet each person by name. Do not spend more than 10 percent of your time getting comfortable. Explain the procedure of the visit. Tell them you will keep an issues sheet handy to allow you to record matters that re-quire further reflection at the end of the visit or in another visit.

Step 3: Read Ephesians 4:17-5:2.

- Open: At what age did your parents let you start choosing what you wore? (Ask Mom or Dad first.) Think about different outfits. What do they tell you about the person? What image do they project? Do clothes make a person?

- Dig: Identity is important for everyone. According to this passage, what is our identity? Who are we to imitate? What do the phrases "put off" and "put on" entail? What attitudes are we to have as Christians? When does anger get bad? When does a joke go wrong? When does talking about people become slander? When does having a good time become debauch-ery? When does making money become greed? What advice does Paul give to help keep us on track? (Don't be partners with immoral persons [Ephesians 5:7], talk to build up, don't let the sun go down on your anger.)

- Reflect: When you think of your personal identity, how does Jesus fit in? Do you believe? If a teen has not made a profession of faith, we ought to ask about personal commitment. Perhaps sharing your own story of coming to faith would be helpful to teens. Is Jesus someone you look up to? Or are you trying to become like a sports or music star?

Step 4: Making commitments is an important way of growing as a Christian. What commitments do you believe God is calling you toward at this time?

Step 5: How can I help you? How can the church help you in your Christian growth?

Step 6: Return to the issues sheet. If you have time, discuss some of these. Add others if necessary. If there are some matters yet to be discussed, arrange for a special meeting. Close in prayer.

Step 7: Write down follow-up items.

Group Discussion: Spiritual Growth

Step 1: Read Philippians 2:1-13. Lead in an opening prayer.

Step 2: Remember what it was like to be a teenager. Here are some questions that can help you think about your life as a teenager:

- What music did you listen to?
- What clothes did you wear?
- How would you rate your self-esteem?
- How influenced were you by your peers?
- What made "old people" seem "old"?

Step 3: Looking at the Christian disciplines, what do you think is different now? The Christian disciplines include prayer, Scripture reading, meditation, study, worship, service, celebration, simplicity, and obedience. (Time will not allow a discussion of all of these.)

- How regularly did you practice the discipline?
- Was it out of habit then? Is it now?
- How does the discipline help you meet God?
- How do you experience God leading you?

Step 4: Give an example of how God has lead you in the past year. How does this help you be more Christlike? How can it lead you toward maturity?

Step 5: In this coming year, what will you do to grow in Christian maturity?

Step 6: Share some items for common prayer. Choose a person to begin the prayer and another to close. Take a few minutes to pray together, allowing time for everyone who wishes to participate.

Group Discussion: Seven Deadly Sins

Step 1: Read Psalm 51. Lead in an opening prayer.

Step 2: The subject for the evening is spiritual growth. Spiritual growth includes at least the following thoughts:

- It is a movement toward maturity in Christ.
- It is a movement toward Christlikeness.
- It is enabled by the work of the Spirit.
- It calls me to act in harmony with God's guidance.

Step 3: Read Philippians 2:12-13. How is God leading you (me) to maturity?

Step 4: Divide a newspaper and/or magazines among the group. Find examples of the seven deadly sins (greed, envy, sloth, pride, lust, gluttony, and anger) as expressed in the media.

Step 5: Listen to Scripture (take the log out of your own eye). In what ways do we find the seven deadly sins come to expression in the church?

Step 6: Remember what it was like to be a teenager. Here are some questions that can help you think about your life as a teenager:

- What music did you listen to?
- What clothes did you wear?
- How would you rate your self-esteem?
- How influenced were you by your peers?
- What made "old people" seem "old"?
- How did your parents try to nurture you?

Step 7: Looking at the seven deadly sins, what do you believe is the difference between then and now? (Time will not allow a discussion of all of these.)

Step 8: Confession of sin is often very routine. How can we make confession (I did it) and contrition (I am sorry) a more meaningful part of our lives?

Step 9: Psalm 51 calls us to pray, "create in me a clean heart, O Lord." What steps can a Christian take to develop "clean" thoughts in a world that promotes "unclean" thoughts?

Step 10: After listening to tonight's discussion, what commitments should we make in our personal and communal life to grow into Christlikeness?

Step 11: Share some items for common prayer. Choose a person to begin the prayer and another to close. Take a few minutes to pray together, allowing time for everyone who wishes to participate.

Go and Learn: Suggestions for Further Reading

Our learning is never completed. The following list of books may help you grow in your understanding. As I read each of these books, I learned a little more about the calling, complexity, and grace of serving God as a spiritual director. My hope is that these authors may serve you equally well.

Spiritual Direction and Congregational Life

Ackerman, John. *Spiritual Awakening: A Guide to Spiritual Life in Congregations.* New York: Alban Institute, 1994.

Barry, William A. and William J. Connolly. *The Practice of Spiritual Direction.* San Francisco: Harper & Row, 1982.

Edwards, Tilden. *Spiritual Friend: Reclaiming the Gift of Spiritual Direction.* New York: Paulist Press, 1980.

Engstrom, Ted. *The Fine Art of Mentoring: Passing On to Others What God Has Given to You.* Brentwood, Tenn.: Wolgemuth & Hyatt, 1989.

Guenther, Margaret. *Holy Listening: The Art of Spiritual Direction.* Boston: Cowley Pub., 1992.

Peterson, Eugene. *The Contemplative Pastor: Returning to the Art of Spiritual Direction.* Grand Rapids, Mich.: Eerdmans, 1989.

Classics of Christian Spirituality

Miller, Calvin. *Walking with Saints.* Nashville: Thomas Nelson Publishers, 1995.

Understanding and Deepening Our Spiritual Lives

Green, Thomas H. *Weeds Among the Wheat: Discernment—Where Prayer and Action Meet.* Notre Dame: Ave Marie Press, 1984.

Ketcham, Katherine, and Ernest Kurtz. *The Spirituality of Imperfection: Storytelling and the Journey to Wholeness.* New York: Bantam Books, 1992.

Muller, Wayne. *Legacy of the Heart: The Spiritual Advantages of a Painful Childhood.* New York: Fireside Press, 1992.

Nouwen, Henri. *Reaching Out: The Three Movements of the Spiritual Life.* New York: Image Books, 1975.

Wicks, Robert J. *Touching the Holy: Ordinariness, Self-Esteem, and Friendship.* Notre Dame: Ave Marie Press, 1992.

——————. *Seeds of Sensitivity: Deepening Your Spiritual Life.* Notre Dame: Ave Marie Press, 1995.

Williams, Clifford. *Singleness of Heart: Restoring a Divided Soul.* Grand Rapids, Mich.: Eerdmans, 1994.

Developing the Practices of Christian Faith

Camelli, Louis, Robert Miller, and Gerard Weber. *A Sense Of Direction: The Basic Elements of the Spiritual Journey.* Valencia, Cal.: Tabor Pub., 1987.

Foster, Richard J. *Celebration of Discipline: The Path to Spiritual Growth.* New York: Harper & Row, 1978.

Green, Thomas H. *Darkness in the Marketplace: The Christian at Prayer in the World.* Notre Dame: Ave Marie Press, 1981.

Groff, Kent Ira. *Active Spirituality: A Guide for Seekers and Ministers.* New York: Alban Institute, 1993.

Postema, Don. *Space For God: The Study and Practice of Prayer and Spirituality.* Grand Rapids, Mich.: CRC Publications, 1983.

Salkin, Jeffrey K. *Being God's Partner: How to Find the Hidden Link Between Spirituality and Work.* Woodstock, Vt.: Jewish Lights Publishing, 1994.

Smith, James Bryan. *A Spiritual Formation Workbook (A Renovare Resource Book).* New York: HarperSanFransico, 1993.

Stevens, R. Paul. *Disciplines of the Hungry Heart: Christian Living Seven Days a Week.* Wheaton, Ill.: Harold Shaw Publishers, 1993.

Tucker, Graham. *The Faith-Work Connection: A Practical Application of Christian Values in the Marketplace.* Toronto: Anglican Book Center, 1987.